BLACK HISTORY,

THE OLD AND NEW

CONTINUES WITH YOU

I0134459

BLACK HISTORY,

THE OLD AND NEW

CONTINUES WITH YOU

SHERELYN DUHART

DUHART PRESS LLC

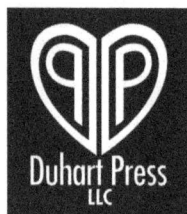

Duhart Press
LLC

Copyright 2016

ISBN: 978-0-9822468-6-3

This book is dedicated to the memory of my mother Maurice Duhart and brother Dwight Duhart.

It is dedicated to my other siblings Courtney, Wana, Teresa, and Derrick.

I would like to acknowledge and thank Sherie Perkins Smith who listened and encouraged me through the journey.

Acknowledgment goes to all friends and readers. Let us make history and create our legacy.

Table of Contents

6

INTRODUCTION

BLACK HISTORY, the old and new, CONTINUES with you.....

Take a journey through old history dating back over seventy five years and journey through new history less than thirty years old. Blacks have created legacies and history that has shaped the world. We have excelled in the arts, sports, literature, education, engineering, scientific inventions, politics, civil rights, the medical field, entertainment and any area you can think of. It's impossible to include everyone in this book, but just the right amount of people to get you energized. This history book has words of inspirations to encourage you to walk in your purpose and fulfil your destiny.

Success is being prosperous and having all of your needs met. It also includes having peace and health. You can have that success in God. God success is righteousness, peace, and joy in the Holy Ghost. Let the peace of God rule in your hearts. It's yours for the asking. I believe that with God all things are possible.

We are a very intelligent and gifted group of people. We play a very significant role in the past, present, and the future. God is no respector of persons. When God created each one of us he created a special person. You are fearfully and wonderfully.

Walk in knowing you are the apple of God's eye. On this journey of life walk in wisdom which comes from God. Martin Luther King said in one of his speeches: There are three dimensions of any complete life- The inward concern that causes one to push forward, to achieve his own goals and ambitions. 2) The outward concern for the welfare of others. 3) The upward reach for God. [i]

We should walk in our purpose which is your legacy. A legacy is anything handed down from the past, as from an ancestor or predecessor.[ii] As we grow and age we need to leave something behind for the person that comes after us.

This chapter in the book of Proverbs is a great proverb to live by.

Something to ponder on as you live day to day:

Proverbs 10

An honest life is Immortal

1 Wise son, glad father;

Stupid son, sad mother,

2 Ill-gotten gain gets you nowhere;

An honest life is immortal.

3 God won't starve an honest soul,

But he frustrates the appetites of the wicked.

4 Sloth makes you poor;

Diligence brings wealth.

5 Make hay while the sun shines-that's smart;

Go fishing during harvest-that's stupid.

6 Blessings accrues on a good and honest life,

But the mouth of the wicked is a dark cave of abuse.

7 A good and honest life is a blessed memorial;

A wicked life leaves a rotten stench.

8 A wise heart takes orders;

An empty head will come unglued.

9 Honesty lives confident and carefree,

But shifty is sure to be exposed.

10 An evasive eye is a sign of trouble ahead,

But an open, face-to-face meeting results in peace.

11 The mouth of a good person is a deep, life –giving well,

But the mouth of the wicked is a dark cave of abuse.

12 Hatred starts fights,

But love pulls a quilt over the bickering.

13 You'll find wisdom on the lips of a person of insight,

But the short-sighted needs a slap in the face.

14 the wise accumulate knowledge- a true treasure;

Know-it-all's talk too much-a sheer waste.

THE Road to Life is a Disciplined Life

15 The wealth of the rich is their bastion;

The poverty of the indigent is their ruin,

16 The wage of a good person is exuberant life;

An evil person ends up with nothing but sin.

17 the road to life is a disciplined life;

Ignore correction and you're lost for good.

18 Liars secretly hoard hatred;

Fools openly spread slander.

19 The more talk, the less truth;

The wise measure their words.

20 the speech of a good person is worth waiting for;

The blabber of the wicked is worthless.

21 the talk of a good person is rich fare for many,

But chatterboxes die of an empty heart[iii]

Wisdom is a great thing; use it as you walk your life out. It's never too late to fulfil your destiny. The people in this book are leaving a legacy or have left a legacy. What is yours? Do you know why God created you? God has created you to be successful. Black history continues with you.

This book is educating, inspiring, and encouraging. It is composed of various areas that our people have excelled in. They are actors, actresses, engineers, scientists, inventors, authors, poets, singers, lawyers, attorneys, surgeons, doctors, musicians, civil rights activists, politicians, artists, sports, singers, publications, ministers, and entrepreneurs.

ACTORS AND ACTRESSES

God knows everything. He knows what he has planned for you. He knew you when you were in your mother's womb. God gives all of us a reason for being on this earth, it's called a purpose. Your purpose could be as simple as being a mother, father, teacher, actor, actress, etc. If God has called you to be an actor or actress, I pray that God will open doors to what you need to be a success. There are various areas you can act in –film, television, or movies.

Doing thing God's way brings peace and joy. You can get to know him. All you have to do is confess and believe in your heart that Jesus died on the cross and rose from the dead.

You may have to start small, do not despise small beginnings. Remain encouraged as you pursue your dreams. Stay focused regardless of the obstacles you may face.

DENZEL WASHINGTON

Denzel came into this world December 28, 1954 in Mount Vernon, New York. His father is a Pentecostal minister and his mother a beautician. He is the middle child of three children. Denzel is married to Paulette. Their children are John David Washington, Olivia Washington, Katia Washington, and Malcom Washington.

Mr. Washington attended Fordham University and majored in journalism. His interest in acting came while performing in drama productions. He moved to San Francisco and enrolled at the American Conservatory Theatre after graduation from college. Denzel is an advocate for the boys and girls club of America.

Denzel has received three Golden Globe Awards, a Tony Award, and two Academy Awards. He made his first appearance on big screen TV in 1981 in the movie *Carbon Copy*. Denzel worked in movies and television during the 80's. He became well known for the role of Dr. Phillip Chandler on *St. Elsewhere*. It aired on NBC and he played the part for six years. Mr. Washington's film career soared when he played the part as Tripp in the movie *Glory* and won an Oscar for best supporting actor.

His acting resume includes:

Equalizer 2014, 2016 *Fences*, 2016 *The Magnificent Seven*, *Flight* 2012, *2 Guns* 2013, *Training Day* 2001, *Safe House* 2012, *The Book of Eli* 2010, *American Gangster* 2007, *Unstoppable*

2010, *Man on Fire* 2004, *Remember the Titans* 2000, *Inside Man* 2006, *The Taking of Pelham* 2009, *Déjà vu* 2006, *John Q 2002,* *Glory* 1989, *The Great Debaters* 2007, *Crimson Tide* 1995, *The Hurricane* 1999, *He Got Game* 1998, *Out of Time* 2003,*Cry Freedom* 1987, *Fallen* 1998, *The Bone Collector* 1999, *Philadelphia* 1993, *Malcom X* 1992, *The Siege* 1996, *The Manchurian Candidate* 2004,*The Pelican Brief* 1993, *Courage Under Fire* 1996, *Virtuosity* 1995, *Antwone Fisher* 2002, *A Soldier's Story* 1984, *The Preacher's Wife* 1996, *Mo' Better Blues* 1990, *Ricochet* 1991, *Devil in a Blue Dress* 1995, *Mississippi Masala* 1991, *Much Ado About Nothing* 1993*, Carbon Copy* 1981, *The Mighty Quinn* 1989, *For Queen and Country* 1989, *License to Kill* 1984, *Heart Condition* 1990, and the list goes on.[iv]

Whatever God has called you to just know: I can do all things through Christ who strengthens you. Romans 8:28. Just lean and trust in God.

SIDNEY POITIER

Sidney L. Poitier was born February 20, 1927 in Miami, Florida. His parents were Reginald James Poitier and Evelyn Poitier. He was married to Juanita Hardy from 1950 to 1965 and married Joanna Shimkus in 1976. His children are Sydney Tamilia Poitier, Sherri Poitier, Anika Poitier, and Beverly Poitier-Henderson. His father was a dirt farmer. Sydney moved to New York at the age of eighteen and worked odd jobs to make ends meet.

Sidney Poitier is known for his role in *Lilies of the Field* and won an Academy Award for Best Actor. He was the first Black American to win a major award. Mr. Poitier is an actor, film director, and author.

His acting resume includes: *In the Heat of the Night* 1967, *Buck and the Preacher* 1972, *The Defiant Ones* 1958, *No Way Out* 1950, *Porgy Bess* 1959, *Stir Crazy* 1980, *To Sir with Love* 1967, *Guess who's coming to Dinner*, *A Raisin in the Sun* 1961*, A Patch of Blue* 1965*, and Lilies of the Field*.

In the *Buck and the Preacher* Film, he played alongside Harry Belafonte. This film marked Poitier's director debut. He also directed *Stir Crazy* with Gene Wilder and Richard Pryor. It was very successful. Mr. Poitier played Thurgood Marshall in *Separate but Equal* in 1991 and played Mandela in *Mandela and DeKlerk* in 1997. He won accolades for playing these famous men.

His written works are *The Measure of a Man: A Spiritual Autobiography, Life Beyond Measure, and This Life.* He has received a Grammy Award for the audio book. Other awards include Presidential Medal of Freedom Award from President Barack Obama. The Chaplain Lifetime Achievement Award was given to him by the Film Society of Lincoln Center in 2011.[v]

Trust in the Lord with all thine heart and lean not until thine own understanding. In all thy ways acknowledge him, and he shall direct thy paths. Proverbs 3:5

EARTHA KITT

On January 17, 1927, Eartha was born in North, South Carolina. She grew up with relatives after her mother abandoned her. Her father was white and her mother was African-American and Cherokee. Her mixed heritage caused her to be teased as a child. At the age of eight, Eartha moved to New York to live with an aunt. Ms. Kitt married John William McDonald. She gave birth to one child, Kitt McDonald.

During her teenage years Ms. Kitt won a scholarship to study with Katherine Dunham and later on she danced with the group. She moved to Paris and became a famous nightclub singer. Orson Welles discovered her while she was in Europe. He thought she was "the most exciting woman alive." In his production, *Dr. Faustus*, he gave her a part as Helen of Troy.

Eartha's Music to name a few: *Eartha Kitt's Songs* 1953, *Down to Earth* 1955, *The Fabulous Eartha Kitt* 1959, *Revisited* 1960, *Bad but Beautiful* 1962, and *The Romantic Eartha* 1962.

Her films/TV appearances are numerous, here are a few: *Friday Foster, The Chastity Belt, Cat Woman, The Protectors, Friday Foster, A Night on the Town, Miami Vice, Living Single, Santa Baby, Living Doll, Matrix, Boomerang, and New York Undercover.*

People know her for a statement she made in 1968 while having lunch with Lady Bird Johnson at the White House. She told the first lady, *You send the best of this country off to be shot and maimed.* Outrage was all over Lady Bird. Kitt's remarks made headlines. The remarks affected her career, and she had to go abroad again. In 1978, she came back to the United States, and starred in a Broadway play entitled *Timbuktu.* Ms. Kitt is best known for her hit *Santa Baby.*

Eartha Kitt believed in working, and she worked until she was in her 70's. President Jimmy Carter invited her to the White House. She received several nominations for her work and won a Daytime Emmy Award for her role in *The Emperor's New School.* The Emmy was for her vocals. She worked at cabarets in New York and was a crowd pleaser. Eartha Kitt died in 2008. Her daughter Kitt has created *Simply Eartha* in honor of her mother and to continue her legacy.[vi]

Then Peter spoke: "I now realize how true it is that God does not show favouritism but accepts men from every nation who fear him and do what is right. Acts 10:34-35 NIV

FRANCES EUGENE HARPER known as HILL HARPER

Hill Harper was born May 17, 1966, in Iowa City, Iowa as Francis Eugene Harper. His parents are Harry Harper and Marilyn Hill. His father is a psychiatrist, and his mother was one of the first black anaesthesiologists in the United States. Frances attended Bella Vista High School, and he graduated in 1984. In the year of 1992 he graduated cum laude from Harvard Law School.

Hill is known for his nine season role as Dr. Sheldon Hawkes on *CSI NY*. He performed as the special agent Spelman Boyle on *Limitless*. Harper is a film, television, and stage actor.

He won the NAACP Image Award for Outstanding Actor in a Drama Series for three consecutive years for his acting position of Dr. Sheldon Hawkes on *CSI NY*. Mr. Harper played in *Covert Affairs* as Calder Michaels.

Hill is the author of several books, *Letters to a Young Brother: Manifest Your Destiny, Letters to a Young Sister: Define your Destiny; The Conversation: How (Black) Men and Women Can Build Loving, Trusting Relationships, The Wealth Cure: Putting Money in Its Place, Letters to an Incarcerated Brother: Encouragement, Hope, and Healing, for Inmates and Their Loved Ones*, and he co-authored *The Badge*. [vii]

And call upon me, and I will answer him Psalm 91:15

LORETTA DEVINE

Loretta grew up in Houston in the Acres Home area. Her mother was a hair stylist and her father James Devine worked as a laborer. Devine graduated from the University of Houston in 1971. She received a Bachelor's of Arts in Speech and Drama and an MFA in Theatre at Brandeis University.

Devine became noticed when she played in *Dreamgirls* on Broadway. Most people know Loretta in the TV series A *Different World*. She played a dormitory director at a fictional Hillman College.

In 1995, she played Gloria Matthews in *Waiting to Exhale*. It was opposite Whitney Houston, Gregory Hines, and Angela Bassett. She won a NAACP Image Award for Outstanding Supporting Actress in a Motion Picture, for *Waiting to Exhale* and *Preacher's Wife*. Her resume includes *This Christmas*, *For Colored Girls* and *Madea's Big Happy Family*.

From 2000 to 2004, Devine starred as a high school teacher Marla Hendricks on the Fox drama series *Boston Public*. Loretta is the winner of three Image Awards for this series.

Other appearances by Ms. Loretta Devine:
The Carmichael Show - Being Mary Jane -The Boris and Nicole Show -Grey's Anatomy-Sirens-Sullivan and Son-Psych -The Client List-The Soul Man- The Game-Shake It Up-State of Georgia-Jumping the Broom-Death at a Funeral-Lottery Ticket-For Colored Girls, Touched by an Angel plus much more.[viii]

Therefore if any man be in Christ, he is a new creature: old things are passed away; behold, all things are become new.

QUEEN LATIFAH

Queen Latifah was born March 18, 1970 in Newark, New Jersey. Her birth name is Dana Elaine Owens. Queen's parents are Lancelot Owens, Sr., and Rita Owens.

Queen Latifah is an American singer, songwriter, rapper, actress, model, television producer, record producer, comedian, and talk show host.

Her musical career projects- *All Hail the Queen*-debut album, *Nature of a Sista*, *Black Reign*, *Order in the Court*, *The Dana Owens Album*, *Trav'lin Light* and *Persona*.

She played on a sitcom entitled *Living Single* from 1993 to 1998 as Khadijah James.

Queen started as a rapper turned actress. Her films include *Set It Off*, *Bringing Down the House*, *Taxi*, *Barbershop2: Back in Business*, *Beauty Shop*, *Last Holiday*, *Hairspray*, *Joyful Noise*, *Miracles from Heaven*, and HBO's *Bessie*.

A television show, entitled *The Queen Latifah Show* is produced and created by the queen. She received her star on Hollywood's Walk of Fame in 2006, a Grammy, an Emmy, a Golden Globe, two Screen Actors Guild Awards, two NAACP Image Awards, and an Academy Award.[ix]

And all things, whatsoever ye shall ask in prayer, believing, ye shall receive. Matthew 21:22

OSSIE DAVIS

Ossie was born Raiford Chatman Davison on December 18, 1917 in Waycross, Georgia. His parents were Laura Davis and Kince Charles Davis; and his children are Hasna Muhammad Davis, Nora Day Davis, and Guy Davis. Ossie attended Howard University for three years before he left to pursue an acting career.

He moved to New York City and worked with the Rose McClendon Players from 1941-1942. The military drafted him and while there he wrote musicals, but returned in 1945 and landed a role in *Jeb* a Broadway production. This is where he met his wife Ruby Dee of over fifty years. They were legends in theatre known as "the first couple of black theatre." Both of them hosted television shows, worked as actors on stage, on screen, radio shows, and television.   The radio show was entitled the Ossie Davis and Ruby Dee Hour. Ossie starred in *Doctor Doolittle* in 1998, *Do the Right Thing* in 1989, and *Butta Ho-Tep* in 2002.

Mr. Davis was active in the civil rights movement. He and his wife were friends with Malcom X, Jesse Jackson, and Martin Luther King Jr.

In 1989, Davis and Dee were inducted into the NAACP Image Awards Hall of Fame. In 1995, they received the National Medal of Arts. It's the nation's highest honor conferred to an artist on behalf of the country. The Kennedy Center honoured them in 2004.

<u>Quotes by Ossie Davis:</u>

Any form of art is a form of power, it has impact, it can affect change –it can not only move us, it makes us move.

I find, in being black, a thing of beauty: a joy, strength; a secret cup of gladness.

Struggle is strengthening. Battling with evil gives us the power to battle evil even more.

Ossie died February 4, 2005 in Miami, Florida.[x]

Therefore I say unto you, what things so ever ye desire, when ye pray, believe that ye receive them, and ye shall have them. Mark 11:24.

ETHEL WATERS

Ethel Waters parents gave birth to her on October 31, 1896. She died in 1977. During her teenage years she sung in Chester, Pennsylvania, singing in the church choir. Touring with the Black Swan Troubadours was a stepping stone for Ethel. There was no contentment with singing jazz and blues; being discontent landed her into acting.

In 1950, Ethel was the first black American to star in her own television show entitled *Beulah*. She won an Emmy Award for her part in the television series *Route 66*. It aired in 1961. The episode *Good Night, Sweet Blues* was the episode that landed the Emmy.

Acting was Ethel's second choice for a career. Her vocal experience includes jazz, blues, pop, and gospel. She was a regular performer on Broadway and earned top billing with her white counterparts.

She claimed notoriety in Hollywood by receiving an Academy Award nomination for the film *Pinky*. Ethel performed at Carnegie Hall in the year of 1938. She had a role in *Cabin in the Sky* in 1943. She starred in *Am I Blue?*, *Memories of You*, *Stormy Weather*, *Porgy*, *Georgia on My Mind*, and *I Can't Give you Anything but Love*.[xi]

By humility and the fear of the Lord are riches, and honour, and life. Proverbs 22:4

CANADA LEE

Canada Lee better known as Bigger Thomas, lived from 1907 to 1951. Mr. Lee is best known for his sensitive portrayal of "Bigger Thomas" the central character in the screen and stage version of Richard Wright's book *Native Son*. Canada Lee never took an acting class. Lee earned rave reviews for this role by Richard Watts in the *New York Herald Tribune*. He declared that his acting was one of the season's (1947) best performances. Before he acted, he played the violin and boxed some. Acting became his true destiny.

Canada won the stage play role Brother Moses. He played in *Stevedore*, *Macbeth*, *Othello*, and *Haiti*, and played a small part in *Mamba's Daughters*. Orson Welles chose him for the Bigger Thomas role. He played roles in *Anna Lucasta*, *South Pacific*, the *Tempest*, a screen version of *Macbeth*, William Saroyan's *Across the Board on Tomorrow Morning*, and in the Tallulah Bankhead picture, *Life Boat*.[xii]

In the house of the righteous is much treasure; but in the revenues of the wicked is trouble. Proverbs 15:6

FREDI WASHINGTON

Fredi Washington was born in Savannah, Georgia and lived from 1903 to 1994. She was an actress. Fredi was a journalist for *People's Voice*. When she was a child, she moved to New York and began her career as a chorus dancer in the stage production of *Shuffle Along* in the year of 1924.

Ms. Washington appeared opposite Paul Roberson in the 1926 play *Black Boy*. After that she left the United States with Al Moire in 1927, and created the dance duo, Moiret and Fredi. They toured clubs in Paris, Monte Carlo, London, and Berlin for two years. She starred in the 1934 film *Imitation of Life*.

Miss Washington stood for equal rights for blacks in the theatre and film industry. In addition, she was a founder of the Negro Actors Guild.[xiii]

Blessed is that man that maketh the Lord his trust, Psalm 40:4

AUTHORS AND POETS

God is no respector of persons. If you believe you have a voice, God is waiting on you. Write, write, and write. Through love serve one another. Let your gift encourage or bless someone. When God gives you a gift, it's never about you.

The Bible talks about, fear not for God is with you. God wants you to act in faith. Without faith it is impossible to please God. Sometimes you have to do it afraid. God honours your actions. God wants to know you trust him. We need authors and poets to create paperbacks, hardbacks, eBooks, write novels, poems, just share your gift with the world.

I hope the authors and poets listed in this section will inspire you to share your voice in writing.

MAYA ANGELOU

Maya Angelou was born Marguerite Annie Johnson, on April 4, 1928 in St. Louis, Missouri. At an early age her parents split up. She and her brother moved to Stamps, Arkansas to live with her father's mother. She was sexually assaulted at seven by her mother's boyfriend while visiting her. Her uncle's killed the guy. Maya was traumatized by the event which caused her to be a mute for several years.

During World War II, Maya moved to California and gave birth to her son, Guy in 1942. In 1952, she wed Anastasios Angelopulos, a Greek sailor. Maya's professional name derived from his name and her childhood nickname "Maya and a shortened version of his surname.

In the 1950's and early 60's Maya was a Broadway and off Broadway actress. She starred in *Porgy and Bess, Calypso Heat Wave,* and *Miss Calypso.* She was a member of the Harlem Writers Guild and a civil rights activist. Angelou starred and created the musical revue *Cabaret for Freedom* as a benefit for the Southern Christian Leadership Conference.

In 1969, she wrote her memoir about her childhood and young adult years, *I Know why the Caged Bird Sings,* it made literary history as the first nonfiction best-seller by an African-American woman. This work made her an international star.

Angelou worked as a composer and writer for singer Roberta Flack. Maya composed movie scores, she wrote articles, short stories, TV scripts, documentaries, autobiographies, poetry, and produced plays. She was a visiting professor for several colleges and universities. A milestone event for Maya was the hit series *Roots*. In 1993, she recited her poem, *On the Pulse of Morning* at President Clinton's inauguration. Maya Angelou died May 28, 2014.

Quotes from Maya Angelou:

I make writing as much a part of my life as I do eating or listening to music. 1999

Nothing so frightens me as writing, but nothing so satisfies me. It's like a swimmer, in the (English) Channel; you face the stingrays and waves and cold and grease and finally you reach the other shore, and you put your food on the ground. 1989

Everyone born comes from the Creator trailing wisps of glory.[xiv]

Psalm 16: 11 Thou will show me the path of life; in thy presence there is fullness of joy; at thy right hand there are pleasures evermore.

JAMES WELDON JOHNSON

Mr. Johnson lived from June 17, 1871 until June 26, 1938. He grew up in Jacksonville, Florida and when he died he domiciled in Wiscasset, Maine.

Mr. Johnson worked as a civil rights activist, writer, composer, politician, educator, and a lawyer. He graduated from Atlanta University. James passed the bar exam, he was a trailblazer, the first Black American to pass the bar in Florida.

During the year of 1906, President Theodore Roosevelt sent him as a representative for the United States to Venezuela and Nicaragua. James Weldon Johnson was the national organizer for the NAACP (National Association for the Advancement of Colored People) in 1920.

James created the Black National Anthem, *Lift every Voice and Sing*. James wrote the first stanza for President Lincoln's Birthday party. It was the year of 1900. His brother John Rosamond helped him create the second stanza, and he composed the song. James Weldon wrote a novel, The *Autobiography of an Ex-Colored Man*. Mr. Johnson edited *The book of American Negro Poetry*. It was a contribution to the history of African- American literature. In addition, he authored a book of poetry, *God's Trombones*.

Mr. Johnson had a talent for persuading people of different backgrounds to come together with one goal in mind. Johnson and his brother wrote over two hundred songs for the Broadway musical stage. James wrote hundreds of poems and stories.

Lyrics to the Black National Anthem

Lift Every Voice and Sing

Lift every voice and sing
Till earth and heaven ring
Ring with the harmonies of Liberty;
let our rejoicing rise,
high as the list'ning skies, let it resound loud as the rolling
sea
sing a song full of faith that the dark past has taught us,
sing a song full of the hope that the present has brought us;
facing the rising sun of our new day begun,
let us march on till victory is won.

Stony the road we trod,
bitter the chastening rod,
felt in the day that hope unborn had died;
yet with a steady beat,
have not our weary feet,
come to the place on witch our fathers sighed?
We have come over a way that with tears has been watered;
we have come, treading our path through the blood of the
slaughtered,

out from the gloomy past, till now we stand at last
where the white gleam of our star is cast.

God of our weary years,
God of our silent tears,
thou who has brought us thus far on the way;
thou who has by thy might,
led us into the light,
keep us forever in the path, we pray
lest our feet stray form the places, our God, where we met
thee,
least our hearts, drunk with the wine of the world, we forget
thee,
shadowed beneath the hand,
may we forever stand,
true to our God,
True to our native land [xv]

Psalm 121:1-2 I will lift up my eyes to the mountains; from
whence shall my help come? My help comes from the Lord.

ZORA NEALE HURSTON

Zora Neale Hurston was born January 7, 1891 in Notasulga, Alabama. Zora Neale worked as an author, an anthropologist, and a folklorist. Ms. Hurston wrote four novels and had more than fifty short stories.

The family moved to Eatonville, Florida when she was three. Mr. Hurston, her father was a Baptist preacher, a farmer, a carpenter, and the mayor of Eatonville.

Ms. Hurston's inspiration for writing began when a Northern schoolteacher came in town and gave her several books. She loved growing up in Eatonville. She loved it so much she wrote an essay about it entitled *How it Feels to be Colored Me.* Her mother died in 1904. Her father remarried, and she attended boarding school but was suspended because of delinquent tuition.

Zora attended Morgan Academy, a division of Morgan College in Baltimore, Maryland. In 1918, she became an undergraduate student at Howard University. She founded the school's newspaper while in attendance. Ms. Hurston was famous for *Their Eyes Were Watching God.*

Several people have written biographies about her. Her hometown has an annual celebration and some of her writings were placed in the Smithsonian Institute. It's the 21st century; Ms. Hurston work is still being used or talked about in film and documentaries.

Just trust God. Psalm 116:2 "I will call on him as long as I live."[xvi]

ARNA BONTEMPS

Arna Bontemps was a prolific writer. His career stretched over three decades. Arna wrote novels, poems, biographies, and published many works in sociology and history. Mr. Bontemps served as a librarian and publicity director at Fisk University in Nashville, Tennessee.

Arna was born October 13, 1902 in Alexandria, Louisiana. He attended the Pacific Union College of California and received a B.A. degree in 1923. He earned a Master's at University of Chicago in 1943 and received numerous awards for his writings. Arna is revered as one of the creative initiators of the Black Renaissance movement of the twenties, a movement that included such artists as Langston Hughes, James Weldon Johnson, Claude McKay, Jean Toomer, Counte Cullen, and several others. In all of his writings, he attempted to portray the richness and variety of the Negro experience in the western hemisphere.

Some of his writings

God Sends Sunday 1931

A Summer Tragedy 1932

Popo and Fifna: Children of Haiti 1932

You Can't Pet a Possum 1934

Black Thunder 1936

Sad Faced Boy 1937

Drums at Dusk 1939

Golden Slippers: An Anthology of Negro Poetry for Young People 1941

The Fast Sooner Hound with Jack Conroy 1942

They Seek a City (with Jack Conroy 1945)

They Have Tomorrow 1945

Sloppy Hooper, The Wonderful Sign Painter 1946

Song of the Negro 1948

The Poetry of the Negro 1746-1949 anthology 1949

George Washington Carver 1950

The Story of George Washington Carver 1954

Frederick Douglas: Slave, Fighter, Free Man [xvii]

Romans 8: 37 NIV In all things we are more than conquerors through him who loved us

<u>TORI DERRICOTTE</u>

Tori Derricotte was born April 12, 1941 in Hamtramck, Michigan. She attended Wayne State University where she earned her BA in special education and obtained her MA in English literature, at New York University.

<u>She has written several books of poetry:</u>

The Undertaker's Daughter

She won the 1998 Paterson Poetry Prize

Captivity

Natural Birth

The Empress of the Death House

The Black Notebooks

<u>Ms. Derricotte honors include:</u>

She won the 1998 Paterson Poetry Prize

Barnes & Noble Writers for Writers Award from poets & Writers

Distinguished Pioneering of the Arts Award from the Unite Black Artists

The Lucille Medwick Memorial Award from the Poetry Society of America.

Fellowships from the Guggenheim Foundation

National Endowment for the Arts

The Rockefeller Foundation

In 2012, Tori Derricotte, was elected Chancellor of the Academy of American Poets in 2012. At the present time she is a professor of English at the University of Pittsburgh.[xviii]

Romans 4:4-5 Now when a man works, his wages are not credited to him as a gift, but as an obligation. However, to the man who does not work but trusts God who justifies the wicked, his faith is credited as righteousness.

RALPH ELLISON

Ralph Waldo Ellison was born March 1, 1914 in Oklahoma City, Oklahoma. Ellison's father, Lewis was an avid reader; he died from an injury at work when Ralph was only three years old. His mother Ida was determined to raise Ralph and his brother Herbert. His mother worked various jobs to survive.

He is known for being an American novelist, scholar, an author, and a literary critic. Mr. Ellison is renowned for his novel *Invisible Man*. This novel was a bestseller. It remained on the bestseller lists for weeks and won the National Book Award and published in 1952

Ellison took up the cornet at an early age and later played the trumpet. He attended Tuskegee Institute in Alabama, while there he studied music and had aspirations of becoming a symphony composer.

In the year of 1936, Ellison went to New York to work and pay for his college. He worked for the New York Federal Writers Program. Mr. Ellison became friends with writers- Richard Wright, Langston Hughes, and Alan Locke who were his mentors. Ellison, published some of his essays and short stories, and worked as managing editor for the *Negro Quarterly*.

Ellison joined the Marines as a merchant cook during World War II. He married Fanny McConnell, and they remained married until his death.

Ellison visited and travelled throughout Europe in the 1950s and lived in Rome for two years and became American Academy fellows. Ellison wrote a book of essays entitled *Shadow and Act* in 1964. He taught at various colleges and universities, which include Bard College and New York University. He wrote *Going to the Territory*, his second collection of essays which was published in 1986. *Juneteenth*, an unfinished novel was published in 1999 after his death. Ellison died in 1994.[xix]

God is full of surprises. You just have to trust him. Ephesians 3:20 Now unto him who is able to do exceeding abundantly above all that we ask or think, according to the power that worketh in us.

RITA DOVE

Rita Dove was born in Akron, Ohio. Her father Ray Dove was the first African-American chemist to work in the US industry as a research chemist at Goodyear. Elvira Hord Dove, her mother earned honors in high school. Ms. Dove shared her passion for reading with her daughter. Rita Dove graduated from high school in 1970 as a Presidential Scholar. She attended Buchtel High School. In 1973, she graduated from Miami University summa cum laude with a B.A.

From 1981 to 1989 she taught creative writing at Arizona State University. In 1987, she won the Pulitzer Prize for poetry. She became the United States Poet Laureate by the Librarian of Congress. Ms. Dove held the position from 1993 to 1995. While serving as poet laureate Bill Moyers featured her on PBS, the *Bill Moyers Journal*.

Poetry collections

Sonata Mulattica, 2009; *American Smooth* 2004; *On the Bus with Rosa Parks* 1999; *Mother Love* 1995; *Selected Poems* 1993; *Grace Notes* 1989; *Thomas and Beaulah* 1986, *Museum 1983*; *The Yellow House on the Corner*, 1980

<u>Essay collection</u> – *The Poet's World* 1995

The Darker Face of the Earth

Through the Ivory Gate 1992[xx]

God knows how to lead and guide you. Psalm 23:2 He maketh me to lie down in green pastures; he leadeth me beside the still waters.

GWENDOLYN BROOKS

Gwendolyn Brooks was born in Topeka, Kansas on June 7, 1917. She is the first child of David Anderson Brooks and Keziah (Wims) Brooks.

Brooks married Henry Lowington Blakely Jr. in 1939.   She gave birth to two children Henry and Nora. She spent all of life in Chicago.

Her poems include *A Street in Bronzeville* (1945), her first volume of poems, which won her the Merit Award for *Mademoiselle Magazine* as the outstanding woman of the year. Mrs; Brooks created her second volume *Annie Allen* (1949), which earned her the Pulitzer Prize for Poetry. Her other major writings include *Bronzeville Boys and Girls* (1956) and (1960). Gwendolyn Brooks wrote a novel entitled *Maude Martha*.

President John Kennedy invited her to read at a Library of Congress poetry festival in 1962. In 1968, she accepted appointment as poet Laureate of Illinois and Poet Laureate of Consultant in poetry to the Library of Congress. Brooks embarked on a teaching career as an instructor in creative writing at Columbia College in Chicago, Chicago State University, Northeastern Illinois University, Columbia University, and the University of Wisconsin.

Poems by Gwendolyn Brooks

A Street in Bronzeville 1945

Annie Allen 1949

The Bean Eaters 1960

In the Time of Detachment, In the Time of Cold 1965

In The Mecca 1968

For Illinois 1968

Riot 1969

Family Pictures 1970

Aloneness 1971

Aurora 1972

Beckonings 1975

Primer for Blacks 1980

To Disembark 1981

Black Love 1982

Mayor Harold Washington; and Chicago, the I Will City 1983

The Near Johannesburg Boy and other Poems 1987

Gottschalk and the Grande Tarantelle 1988

Winnie 1988

Children Coming Home 1991

In Montgomery, and other Poems 2003

Gwendolyn died December 3, 2000.[xxi]

Proverbs 29:18 Where there is no vision the people perish: but he that keepeth the law happy is he.

ENGINEERS/INVENTORS/ SCIENTISTS

If you have the desire to be an engineer, inventor, or scientist know that you can do all things through Christ who strengthens you. You have the mind of Christ.

Science knowledge has allowed us to call people on a cell phone, vaccinate a baby against polio, build buildings, and drive cars. We need scientist because science helps us answer important questions. Some of the questions are how we can protect crops from pests, what areas might be hit by a tsunami, and questions about the ozone layer.

Make your own history by becoming a scientist and help the society answer questions that need to be answered.

Engineers apply science knowledge, mathematics, and ingenuity to develop solutions for technical, social, and commercial problems. Black engineers are needed in all of these areas. It is your turn to make history.

Inventors are creative. They see new possibilities, connections, or relationships that spark an invention.

The world needs scientists, inventors, and engineers –much success to you as you make your mark in history.

RON MCNAIR

Ronald McNair, an astronaut, was born October 21, 1950 in Lake City, South Carolina. Ron was radical at a young age he refused to leave a library when they would not allow him to check out his books. The police and his mother was called, after they arrived he could check out his book. The library is named after him now. Mr. McNair graduated from Carver High School and earned the right to be valedictorian in the year of 1967.

He received a bachelor's degree in engineering physics, graduated magna cum laude, from North Carolina A & T State University in Greensboro, North Carolina. Ron attended Massachusetts Institute of Technology in 1976. He got a Ph.D. in physics. Mr. McNair was known for his work in laser physics.

After graduating from MIT, he worked as a staff assistant at Hughes Research Laboratories in Malibu, California. In 1978, he was selected as an astronaut candidate. He graduated from a one year training and evaluation period in August 1979; this qualified him for assignments as a mission specialist astronaut on Space Shuttle flight crews.

Ron had two missions as an astronaut. On his first mission he logged 191 hours in space.

On the last one he planned to take part in a saxophone recording on the challenger. The Challenger was his last mission. The Challenger disintegrated only nine miles above the Atlantic Ocean less than two minutes after take-off. He died on January 28, 1986 aboard this   Challenger mission.

Honors and Awards

- Willowridge High School in Houston has a building on campus in honor of McNair.

- There is a memorial in the Ronald McNair Park in Brooklyn, New York.

- The Dr. Ronald E. McNair Playground in East Harlem, New York is named after him.

- The Ronald E. McNair Space Theater inside the Davis Planetarium in downtown Jackson, Mississippi is named in his honor.

- The Naval ROTC building on the campus of Southern University and A&M College in Baton Rouge, Louisiana is named in his honor.

- Ronald E. McNair Hall is on the campus of North Carolina A&T State University in Greensboro, NC.

- The Engineering building at North Carolina A&T State University in Greensboro, North Carolina is named in his honor.

- The McNair Post-baccalaureate Achievement Program, which operates at 179 campuses in the U.S. (April 7), awards research money and internships to first-generation and otherwise under-represented students in preparation for graduate work

- McNair portrayed by Joe Morton in the 1990 TV movie *Challenger*.

- The song, "A Drop of Water," recorded by Japanese jazz artist Keiko Matsui, with vocals by the late Carl Anderson, wrote a tribute to McNair.

- The Jean Michel Jarre track "Last Rendez-Vous" retitled "Ron's Piece" in his honor. McNair scheduled to record the track in space aboard Challenger and then perform it via a live link up in Jarre's Rendez-vous Houston concert.[xxii]

To walk in your purpose, you have to do your part. Hebrews 11:1 Now faith is the substance of things hoped for; the evidence of things hoped for, the evidence of things not seen.

JAMES WEST

Mr. West was born in Prince Edward County, Virginia on February 10, 1931. He graduated from Temple University with a Bachelor's Degree in Physics in 1957. James West, Ph.D., was a Bell Laboratories Fellow at Lucent Technologies where he specialized in electro, physical, and architectural acoustics. His research in the early 1960s led to the development of foil-electret transducers for sound recording and voice communication used in ninety percent of all microphones built today and at the heart of most new telephones being manufactured.

James West holds forty-seven US patents and more than two hundred foreign patents on microphones and techniques for making polymer foil-electrets. He has authored more than one hundred papers and contributed to books on acoustics, solid state physics, and material science. West has received numerous awards including the Golden Torch Award in 1998 sponsored by the National Society of Black Engineers. He received the Lewis Howard Latimer Light Switch and Socket Award in 1989, and chosen as the New Jersey Inventor of the Year for 1995.[xxiii]

If ye abide in me, and my words abide in you, ye shall ask what ye will, and it shall be done unto you. John 15:7

MARJORIE JOYNER

Marjorie Joyner was born October 24, 1896 in Monterey, Virginia. She was the granddaughter of a slave and a slave-owner. Her desire was to move to Chicago to pursue a career in cosmetology. Ms. Joyner attended the A.B. Molar Beauty School in 1916 and was the first Black women to graduate from the school. After graduation, she married a podiatrist, Robert E. Joyner. Soon after that, she opened a beauty salon.

Marjorie Joyner was an employee of Madame C J Walker. Ms. Joyner became famous when she invented a permanent wave machine, which created long and lasting hair styles in a wave pattern. The wave machine was patented in 1928. It was popular amongst whites and blacks. Marjorie never became financial successful as a result of inventing the machine because it became the property of the Walker Company. Madame Walker owned the rights to the machine.

Ms. Joyner was the Director of Madame Walker's beauty schools. She and Mary McLeod Bethune founded the United Beauty School Owners and Teachers Association in 1945. Marjorie founded the Alpha Chi Pi Omega Sorority and Fraternity to raise the standards of beauticians. Bethune-Cookman College awarded her a psychology degree in 1973 at the age of 77.

During the depression, Ms. Joyner volunteered for non-profit/charities that provided lodging, education, and work for African Americans.

Mrs. Joyner died at the age of ninety-eight on December 7, 1994. Her legacy includes creativity, ingenuity, and selflessness.[xxiv]

Psalms 46:10 Be still and know that I am God.

LLOYD AUGUSTA HALL

Mr. Hall was born June 20, 1894 in Elgin, Illinois. Lloyd's father Augustus, was a minister, and his mother Isabel, a homemaker.

Lloyd invented Chemical Products Corporation in 1922; it was a food science consulting firm.

Lloyd Augusta Hall invented curing salts for the meatpacking industry. The salts were created when he worked as chief chemist and director of research for Griffith Laboratories in Chicago. Mr Hall worked for Griffith for thirty four years. He received a patent in 1951 for the process. It cured bacon in several hours instead of the six to eighteen days it would take others.

Lloyd graduated from Northwestern University and received a Bachelor of Science degree in pharmaceutical chemistry. He earned a M.S. degree from the University of Chicago. Mr Hall received approximately twenty five patents for the manufacturing and packing industry.

He died January 2, 1971.[xxv]

Proverbs 9:10 NASB The fear of the Lord is the beginning of wisdom, and the knowledge of the Holy One is understanding.

BESSIE COLEMAN

Bessie was born on January 26, 1892 in Atlanta, Texas. Her father was George Coleman. He moved to Oklahoma in 1901 and lived in the Indian Territory.

Bessie graduated from eighth grade with high marks. After that she attended an industrial college in Oklahoma. Bessie read about the field of aviation and her interest heightened when her brothers told her stories about French women flying planes in World War I.

Bessie Coleman was the first black female to fly. Believe it or not, she was prevented from attending flight school in the United States. Mrs. Coleman enrolled in flight school in France and studied the science of aviation. She flew in many flight exhibitions, which assisted in paying for her flight school. Unfortunately, her dream of her own flight school was short lived; she died in a plane crash before her dream could be realized.

She died April 30, 1926.[xxvi]

Not by might, nor by power, but by my spirit, saith the Lord. Zechariah 4:6

MEREDITH CHARLES GOURDINE

Meredith Charles "Flash" Gourdine came into the world September 26, 1929 in Newark, New Jersey, and he was the first inventor to use electrogasdynamics (EGD) to make useful inventions. EGD is the generation of electricity through the energy in highly pressurized gases. His father instilled a strong work ethic in him; he worked as a painter and janitor during his early years.

Meredith attended Brooklyn Technical High School and worked with his father after school. His father encouraged him to get an education so he would not have to be a laborer all his life. He heeded his father's advice. He played sports and received a scholarship for swimming at the University of Michigan; he turned it down and attended Cornell University instead. Mr. Gourdine earned his bachelor's degree in engineering in 1953 and he was an officer in the United States Navy

In 1964, Mr. Gourdine borrowed $200,000.00 from friends and family and he opened up Gourdine Laboratories located in Livingston, New Jersey. Meredith employed over 150 employees. The talented and intelligent Mr. Gourdine founded Energy Innovation in Houston, Texas; this company produced direct energy conversion devices.

Another big accomplishment was the creation of the incineraid system, which was used to disperse smoke from burning buildings and used to disperse fog on airport runways.

He held over thirty patents and in 1994 he was inducted into the Engineering and Science Hall of Fame.

Mr. Gourdine died November 20, 1998. He left behind a legacy of design, research, and innovation.[xxvii]

Never give up be patient. Psalm 62:5 My soul, wait thou only upon God.

GARRETT AUGUSTA MORGAN

Mr. Morgan was born in Paris, Kentucky on March 4, 1877. Garrett received a sixth grade education. His father was the son of a slave and a Confederate colonel, John Hunt Morgan. Garrett's mother was half Indian and Black. Her father was a Baptist minister.

In his mid-teens he moved to Cincinnati, Ohio. Morgan worked at sewing-machine factories and learned the trade. Mr. Morgan received a patent for improving the sewing machine. As a result, he opened up his own sewing machine repair shop. Mr. Garrett married Mary Anne Hassek and together they had three sons. His wife had experience as a seamstress.

Garrett Morgan established a hair company called G.A. Morgan Hair Refining Company and sold his cream product to African Americans.

Mr. Garrett was the first black man in Cleveland to own a car. He was so talented he developed a friction drive clutch.

One of his greatest inventions was the gas mask and protection hood in 1912. This enabled firefighters to enter smoky or toxic environments. Mr. Morgan's mask saved the lives of hundreds of American soldiers during World War I. White salesmen sold his mask. People found out a black man invented the mask people stopped buying it.

The red light/green light that we use today was developed first by

Mr. Morgan. His invention was a tall pole with a bell on top and two flags with stop printed on them, the signal was controlled by raising and lowering the flags by rotating a hand crank near the base of the mechanism. He received a US patent on November 20, 1923. General Electric paid him 40,000 for the rights of his automatic stop sign.

Garrett Augustus Morgan Sr. died on July 27, 1963. He was in Cleveland, Ohio.[xxviii]

God gives you friends that will encourage you. Proverbs 11:14 Where no counsel is, the people fall: but in the multitude of counsellors there is safety.

DENNIS WEATHERBY

Dennis Weatherby, PHD was born December 4, 1959, and died September 15, 2007. He grew up in Brighton, Alabama and graduated from Midfield High School. Weatherby attended Central State University in Wilberforce, Ohio; while there he earned a bachelor's degree in chemistry in 1982. After that he moved to the University of Dayton and received a master's degree in chemical engineering in 1984. After he finished receiving his degrees, he worked for Proctor & Gamble in Cincinnati, Ohio as a process engineer.

He was a scientist, an inventor, university administrator, and a supporter of minority children. Mr. Weatherby got a patent on lemon scented Cascade, while he worked at Procter & Gamble. He was the director of Auburn University's Minority Engineering Program. Mr. Weatherby made Auburn one of the top universities for graduating African Americans in engineering.

In 1989, he worked for his alma mater, CSU as an academic advisor and recruiter in the water resources center. While there Weatherby helped increase the student enrollment, it grew at four hundred percent. In 2004, Weatherby became an associate dean of the graduate school at the University of Notre Dame. He worked at Northern Kentucky University as an associate Provost in 2006. He served there until his death.[xxix]

James 1:9 NASB This you know, my beloved brethren. But let everyone be quick to hear, slow to speak and slow to anger.

JESSE EUGENE RUSSELL

Jesse Eugene Russell was born April 26, 1948 in Nashville, Tennessee. He attended Tennessee State University and Stanford University; he majored in electrical engineering. Russell has been extremely instrumental in shaping the wireless industry to what it is today. Russell invented digital cellular technology and developed many patents and regularly continues to invent new technology for emerging technology for wireless networks known as 4G. The Clinton Administration inducted him into the United States Academy of Engineering for his invention of digital cellular technology.

Mr. Russell grew up in Nashville with his parents and eight sisters/ brothers. The turning point for Russell's destiny was when he attended a summer educational program at Fisk University. After graduating from college, Russell was the first African American to work for AT & T Bell companies in Nashville. He was an honor student at TSU and elected to Eta Kappa Nu Outstanding Young Electrical Engineer of the year in 1980. Mr. Russell is a man to be proud of.

Some of his patents:

1. Advanced multi-network client device for wideband multimedia access to private and public wireless networks.
2. Broadband cable telephony network architecture IPITN network architecture reference model.
3. Wireless communication base station.

4. Wireless terminal having digital radio processing with automatic communication system selection capability.
5. Wireless communication system having base units which extracts channel and setup information from nearby base units.
6. Mobile data telephone.
7. Base station for mobile radio telecommunications systems

These are just a few of his patents.

Russell is creditworthy for AT&T's growth of broadband communication network. He specialized in cable access networks, DSL Access Networks, Powerline-Carrier Access Networks, Fixed Wireless Access Networks, Satellite Access Networks and Broadband Wireless Communications Network.[xxx]

Praying all the time helps. Philippians 4:6-7 NIV Do not be anxious about anything, but in everything by prayer and petition, with thanksgiving, present your requests to God. And the peace of God, which transcends all understanding, will guard your hearts and your minds in Christ Jesus.

GEORGE WASHINGTON CARVER

George Washington Carver, a scientist of the past, born in 1864 grew up in Southwest Missouri where he worked as a farm hand. His father Moses Carver was a slave. Mr. Carver attended Iowa Agricultural College, known as Iowa State College and Simpson College in Indianola, Iowa; he studied piano during this time. He had an interest in farming and planting at an early age. George did not start college until he was thirty.

George Washington Carver was a miracle sent from God; he used peanuts to rescue the farmers of his day. Booker T. Washington convinced Carver to come to Tuskegee Institute to serve as the schools director of Agriculture. This is where Carver created his crop rotation method which changed and saved the agriculture in the south. Mr. Carver encouraged the farmers to grow other products than cotton.

Slavery was going away, so the farmers needed an emergency solution. Farmers grew peanuts, peas, soybeans, sweet potatoes, and pecans. God sent Carver, and he knew God sent him. Carver did not patent or profit from his invention. He changed the South from being a one-crop farmer to being a multi crop farmer.

In 1940 Carver donated his life savings to establish the Carver Research Foundation at Tuskegee for continuing research in agriculture.

Honors

He received an honorary doctorate from Simpson College in 1928. He was an honorary member of the Royal Society of Arts in London, England.

1923- Springarn Medal from the NAACP

1939 Roosevelt Medal for restoring Agriculture in the South

July 14, 1943 President Roosevelt honored him with a national monument dedicated to his accomplishments.

Diamond Grove Missouri has a park preserved and was the first designated national monument to an African American.[xxxi]

Just believe, Mark 9:23 Jesus said unto him. "If thou canst believe, all things are possible to him that believeth."

GRANVILLE T. WOODS

Granville T. Woods was born in Columbus, Ohio, in 1856. Mr. Woods dedicated his life to developing a variety of inventions relating to the railroad industry. To some he was known as the "Black Edison". Woods invented more than a dozen devices to improve electric railway cars. His most noted invention was systems for letting the engineer of a train know how close his train was to others. This device helped cut down accidents and collisions between trains.

Alexander Graham Bell's company purchased the rights to Woods' "telegraphony," enabling him to become a full-time inventor. Among his other top inventions were a steam boiler furnace and an automatic air brake used to slow or stop trains. Wood's electric car was powered by overhead wires. It was the third rail system to keep cars running on the right track.

Success led to law suits filed by Thomas Edison. Woods won, but Edison did not give up when he wanted something. Trying to win Woods over, and his inventions, Edison offered Woods a prominent position in the engineering department of Edison Electric Light Company in New York. Woods, preferring his independence, declined.[xxxii]

Get to know God, follow him. He has great plans for you. John 8:12 NIV I am the light of the world. Whosoever follows me will never walk in darkness, but will have the light of life.

FREDERICK MCKINLEY JONES

Mr. Jones was born in Covington, Kentucky on May 17, 1893. Frederick served in World War I. Upon returning home he worked as a garage mechanic. After gaining this experience he created and developed a self-starting gasoline motor.
His expertise in electronic devices was self-taught through his work experience and his inventions. His jobs soon after the garage included working on a steamboat and at a hotel.

Following these job assignments he moved to Hallock, Minnesota. He began to build race cars and drove them at local tracks and county fairs. His car was known as Number fifteen, it was so well designed that it defeated an airplane.

Mr. Jones invented a silent movie projector and a machine to return change to movie customers. Frederick continued to create and invent; he invented a snowmobile.

He is the inventor of keeping trucks refrigerated while traveling the highways. His invention kept food frozen. Before his invention the food froze by packing them with ice. Mr. Jones won the National Medal of Technology award in 1991 and was the first black to receive this honor. In the field of refrigeration he had forty patents. He elysian'd to create refrigerated transportation when a truck driver lost his truck load of chickens because he did not make it to the destination before the ice melted.

Before his death on February 21, 1961, he had sixty inventions.[xxxiii]

For whatever you need in life, the word of God says, Pray without ceasing. I Thessalonians 5:17.

DR. MAE C. JEMISON

Dr. Mae C. Jemison's legacy includes being a medical doctor and an astronaut.

Dr. Mae C. Jemison was born October 17, 1956 in Decatur, Alabama. She graduated from Stanford University in 1977. Dr. Jemison received a doctor of science in chemical engineering. Ms. Jemison attended medical school at Cornell University. Mrs. Jemison received a grant from the International Traveling Institute for health studies and went to Africa in January 1983 where she worked as a medical area peace specialist.

After the space challenger explosion, she applied for a position as an astronaut. In 1987, she earned a position into the astronaut program. In 1992, she flew on the shuttle Endeavor, a joint project of Japan and the United States. She left NASA in 1993.

Dr. Jemison developed and participated on research projects on Hepatitis B vaccine, schistosomaisis, and rabies in conjunction with the National Institute of Health and the Center for Disease Control.

Mrs. Jemison's experience includes:

Internship at Los Angeles County/USC Medical Center -July 1982

General Practitioner with INA/Ross Loos Medical Group in Los Angeles -was there until December 1982

Area Peace Corps Medical Officer Sierre Leone and LIberia in West Africa- from January 1983 to June 1985

Cigna Health Plans of California -1985

In 1993, she formed her own company, The Jemison Group.

Jemison founded the Dorothy Jemison Foundation for Excellence, named in honor of her mother.

Books by Jemison:

The 100 year Starship

Discovering New Planets

Journey through our Solar System

Exploring our Sun along with Dana Meachen [xxxiv]

Looking unto Jesus the author and finisher of our faith. Hebrews 12:2

SURGEONS/DOCTORS

God bless you and keep you as you serve or prepare to serve your patients. You can be sure that God will take care of everything you need, his generosity exceeding even yours in the glory that pours from Jesus. Philippians 4:19. To become a doctor it takes commitment and dedication. Being a surgeon or doctor requires hard work and numerous study hours. Remain focus. You can do all things through Christ who strengthens you. It may be hard but do not give up. If you desire to be a surgeon, gynecologists, pediatrician, ophthalmologist, orthopedist, neurosurgeon, neurologist, etc., you can do whatever you put your mind to.

There was a physician in the Bible named Luke.

Colossians 4:14 Our dear friend, Luke, the doctor, and Demas send greetings.

Luke was a doctor by trade before he was called to be a disciple. Luke accompanied Paul on his journeys and used his medical skills to assist him.

I pray that God will provide all the finances you need, you will make the grades, and have a successful career as a doctor.

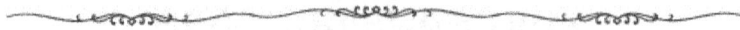

If your journey in life is to become a surgeon, He took good care of them, they had nothing to fear. Psalms 78: 53-55

DR. PATRICIA BATH

Dr. Patricia Bath was born November 4, 1942 in New York City, New York in the Harlem area.

Doctor Patricia Bath is an ophthalmologist and laser scientist. Ms. Bath was the first African American female doctor to patent a medical invention. Her patent removes a cataract lens that transforms eye surgery by using a laser device.

Cataract Laserphaco Probe -Patricia Bath's dedication and passion led her to develop treatment and prevention of blindness. She developed the Cataract Laserphaco Probe, which was patented in 1988. It used the power of a laser to vaporize cataracts from patients' eyes.

Bath created another invention that restores sight to people who have been blind for over thirty years. Ms. Bath's inventions are used all over the world in places such as Japan, Canada, Europe, and of course the United States.

Other Achievements:

In 1968, Patricia Bath graduated from the Howard University School of Medicine. She completed specialty training in ophthalmology and corneal transplant at both New York University and Columbia University.

In 1975, Bath became the first African-American woman surgeon at the UCLA Medical Center and the first woman to be on the faculty of the UCLA Jules Stein Eye Institute.

Dr. Bath founded and served as the first president of the American Institute for the Prevention of Blindness.

Patricia Bath elected to Hunter College Hall of Fame in 1988 and elected as Howard University Pioneer in Academic Medicine in 1993.

Her Greatest Obstacle:

per Dr. Bath: *Sexism, racism, and relative poverty were the obstacles which I faced as a young girl growing up in Harlem. There were no women physicians I knew of and surgery was a male-dominated profession; no high schools existed in Harlem, a predominantly black community; blacks excluded from numerous medical schools and medical societies; and, my family did not possess the funds to send me to medical school.*[xxxv]

God thinks highly of you. He made you in his likeness. Genesis 1:26 And God said, Let us make man in our image, after our likeness.

DANIEL HALE WILLIAMS III

Daniel Hale Williams was born January 18, 1856 in Hollidaysburg, Pennsylvania. Mr. Hale's parents were Daniel Hale Williams II and Sarah Price Williams. Daniel was the eldest of several children. His father was a barber. Daniel entertained the barbering business for a while but lost interest.

Mr. Hale worked as an apprentice for Dr. Henry Palmer. Later on he went to medical college at Chicago Medical College.

Daniel Hale III founded the Provident Hospital and Training School May 4, 1892. Mr. William's legacy includes performing the first successful open heart operation. On July 9, 1893 a man came to the hospital after being stabbed in the chest during a bar brawl. Williams opened a small trapdoor in the patient's chest, assessed the wound, repaired the damage to the left internal mammary artery, and closed a second wound in the quivering pericardium which covered the heart. The patient marked healthy and discharged fifty-one-days later. Williams wanted nurses black and white to be trained with high standards. He made sure training for doctors, especially black surgeons, improved.

In 1893, he married Alice Johnson they lived in Chicago. Daniel continued his work at Provident, and worked at Cook County Hospital and St. Luke Hospital

Dr. Hale was a volunteer visiting physician to Meharry Medical College for more than two decades.

Dr. Daniel Hale Williams III died August 4, 1931.[xxxvi]

Psalm 37:7 Rest in the Lord, and wait patiently for him.

Dr. LOUIS TOMPKINS WRIGHT

Louis T. Wright was born in LaGrange, Georgia on July 23, 1891. Mr. Wright followed in his father's footsteps, his father was a doctor. Dr. Louis graduated from Clark University in 1911 and graduated from Harvard University's School of Medicine in 1915; he was fourth in his class.

Louis Wright wrote columns for the NAACP magazine *Crisis,* he began the publication of the scholarly *Harlem Hospital Bulletin*, and established the hospital's medical library.

He was the first black physician to be appointed to the staff of a New York hospital. Wright had successful work in the army with a small pox vaccination using an injection method rather than the scratching method.

In 1948, Dr. Wright entered the field of cancer research and founded the Harlem Hospital Cancer Research Foundation. It dealt with the effectiveness of chemotherapeutic agents to attack and destroy cancer cells.

The ultimate achievement of Dr. Wright occurred in 1949, when he became the first physician in the world to experiment on humans with the drug Aureomycin. This drug cured typhus, pneumonia, and intestinal infections. He published thirty papers on his discoveries with Aureomycin. Dr. Wright is also credited with developing the neck brace used to care for patients with a broken neck without moving the person and causing further damage to the spinal cord. He also invented a blade plate for surgical treatment of fractures.

Dr. Wright died on October 8, 1952.[xxxvii]

You trust God, he is faithful. Psalm 119:105 Thy word is a lamp unto my feet, and a light unto my path.

PERCY LAVON JULIAN

Percy Julian was born on April 11, 1899 in Montgomery, Alabama; his legacy was valuable contributions to organic chemistry and arthritis. The grandson of a former slave, Julian received an inadequate education at the segregated schools of Alabama. He entered DePauw University in 1916 and graduated valedictorian in 1920. Julian was forced to take remedial classes to make up for the deficiencies in the Alabama school system. Julian was a tireless worker.

Julian accepted a teaching position at Fisk University and remained there until he won the Austin Fellowship in Chemistry position at Harvard University. He served at Howard University and travelled to Vienna and earned a PH. D in organic chemistry.

Dr. Julian developed inexpensive copies of many drugs, making them accessible to the population. In 1935 he developed an exact copy of the rare and expensive drug used to treat glaucoma. Julian created synthetic cortisone, which cost several hundred dollars less per gram to produce than the cortisone. This reduced the cost of treating arthritis and other muscle and bone disorders.

In 1953, Dr. Julian opened his own research firm, Julian Laboratories, and founded Julian Associates and the Julian Research Institute in 1964. Julian's company flourished he made millions making synthetic steroids. Before he died he had more than one hundred patents.

Dr. Julian died on April 19, 1975.[xxxviii]

If you're called to be a housewife, doctor, nurse etc. God will see you through whatever you do. Philippians 1:6 NIV Being confident of this, that he who began a good work in you will carry it on to completion until the day of Christ Jesus.

CHARLES DREW

Charles Drew was born in Washington, DC on June 3, 1904. He had four siblings Elsie Drew, Eva Drew, Nora Drew, and Joseph Drew. He married Minnie Lenore Robbins in 1939, and they gave birth to Charlene Drew Jarvis and Charles Drew Jr.

Charles Drew was the first African American to receive the doctor of science degree in medicine and receive his bachelor's degree at Amherst College in 1925. He graduated from McGill University Medical School in Canada in 1933.

Drew did research at Columbia University on blood preservation. Drew discovered that plasma, or blood fluid with the cells and platelets separated out, was much easier to preserve than whole blood.

Mr. Drew wrote a thesis on "Banked Blood," In his thesis he addressed evolving of the blood bank, the transformation that occur in preserved blood, and successfully pioneered methods of storing blood plasma. The blood bank was established at Presbyterian Hospital (New York City) in August 1939 by him and Dr. John Scudder.

Charles Drew died April 1, 1950 in Burlington, North Carolina.[xxxix]

Through the journey, please know that God will see you through. Psalm 46: 1 God is our refuge and strength, a present help in trouble.

WILLIAM AUGUSTUS HINTON

William Hinton was born in Chicago, Illinois on December 15, 1883. Hinton received fame for developing a test for syphilis; it was named the Davis-Hinton test for syphilis detection. He attended Harvard University as an undergraduate and graduated from medical school in 1912, but could not get an internship because of his race.

Dr. Hinton secured a position at Wasserman Laboratory, as the assistant director in 1915. While there he became an authority in venereal disease worldwide. Hinton authored a book in 1936, *Syphilis and its Treatment*. It was the first medical textbook published by a black American. In 1949, Hinton taught at Harvard, he was the first Black American to teach there.

The U.S. Public Health Service came to admit that Hinton's test was the most efficient for early detection of the disease.

In 1931, he started a school at the Boston Dispensary to train men and women to become laboratory technicians. It grew into one of the largest school's for medical technician training. This program continues today at Northeastern University in Boston. Graduates of the school are hired nationwide by laboratories and hospitals.

Mr. Hinton was a very modest man. He earned the NAACP's Spingarn Medal in 1938. Mr. Hinton refused it because he felt like he had not done enough.

Dr. Hinton died August 8, 1959 in Canton, Massachusetts.[xl]

Hebrews 2:13 I will put my trust in him.

CIVIL RIGHTS ACTIVIST

Civil rights activist for everyone will be needed until Jesus returns. The activists of the past prayed and worked hard; they set out to finish their mission. The activists of today have to work the same way. It takes courage to be civil rights activists. The fight continues and cannot be fought the same as the past was fought. In the past, people were sprayed by water hoses, spit at, etc. It takes faith to fight against discrimination based on race, color, religion, sex, or national origins. God loves everyone, and he states love covers a multitude of sin. Trusting God will help you fight the battle. God is a god of justice and righteousness. May God be with you if you're called to be an activist. I pray the angels of the Lord be encamped about you.

I Corinthians 16:13, 14 Be on your guard, stand firm in the faith, be courageous, be strong. Do everything in love.

ROY WILKINS

Roy Wilkins was the senior statesman of the Civil Rights Movement, born on August 30, 1901 in St. Louis, Missouri. Mr. Wilkins was known for his leadership role in the NAACP – National Association for the Advancement of Colored People. His mother died when he was four. He was raised by his aunt and uncle in St. Paul, Minnesota. Wilkins graduated from the University of Minnesota with a degree in sociology in 1923.

After graduation, Wilkins worked as a journalist at *The Minnesota Daily* and became editor of *THE APPEAL* an African –American newspaper. He was assistant NAACP secretary under Walter Francis Whitt. Mr. Wilkins became the editor of the *Kansas City Call*. In the year of 1929, he married Aminda "Minnie" Badeau. The couple did not give birth to any children.

Roy Wilkins, A. Philip Randolph (founder of the Brotherhood of Sleeping Car Porters), and Arnold Aronson (leader of the National Jewish Community Relations Advisory Council) founded the Leadership Conference on Civil Rights (LCCR). It's the premier organization for the civil rights movement. This organization is responsible for national drives and created civil rights laws since 1957.

One milestone for Wilkins was, being instrumental in getting money deposited into Tri-State Bank in Memphis, Tennessee so that credit worthy blacks could get lines of credit. By 1955, the bank deposits totalled $280,000.

Roy Wilkins was chosen to be the executive secretary of the NAACP and in 1964 became its executive director and had an excellent reputation as an articulate spokesperson for the civil rights movement.

Roy Wilkins was an advocate of achieving reform through the legislature. He testified before many Congressional hearings and conferred with Presidents Kennedy, Johnson, Nixon, Ford, and Carter.

He was awarded the Spingarn Medal from the NACCP in 1964. President Lyndon Johnson awarded him the Presidential Medal of Freedom during his tenure. He also spearheaded the Brown v Board of Education, the Civil Rights Act of 1964, and the Voting Rights Act of 1965.

Roy Wilkins died on September 9, 1981. His autobiography was published in 1982, *Standing Fast: The Autobiography of Roy Wilkins*.[xli]

And I say unto you, Ask, and it shall be given you; seek, and ye shall find; knock, and it shall be opened unto you. Luke 11:9

WHITNEY MOORE YOUNG JR.

Whitney Young Jr., a civil rights activist served with Martin Luther King, James Farmer, Roy Wilkins, A Phillip Randolph, and John Lewis. They were the forefront members of the Civil Rights' movement. Whitney Young came into the earth on July 31, 1921 in Lincoln Ridge, Kentucky. His mother was a teacher and his father a principal. Whitney attended Kentucky State Industrial College. Mr. Young married his college sweetheart, Margaret Buckner. The couple had two children.

Mr. Young served as the executive director of the Urban League in 1961 and he managed its expansion. The League played a major part in integrating staff and employees for several big companies. He oversaw the racial integration of corporate workplaces. Whitney Young Jr. attended Kentucky State Industrial College. The Urban League was a co-sponsor of the historic 1963 March on Washington.

In the year of 1950, Young became the executive secretary of the Omaha, Nebraska branch that was in the heat of racial tension. During the mid-fifties, Whitney Young took a position as the dean of Social Work at Atlanta University. His passion for the civil rights movement continued in Atlanta, he headed up the NAACP branch for the state of Georgia.

Whitney worked as a teacher before he served in World War II. While on active duty he acted as a bridge between black and white servicemen. After the war, Young earned his master's degree from the University of Minnesota in Social Work. In the political arena, Young was a close adviser to Lyndon B. Johnson. In addition, he received the Presidential Medal of Freedom in 1968.

Young authored two books- *To Be Equal* 1964 and *Beyond Racism: Building an Open Society* 1969.

Young died March 11, 1971 in Lagos, Nigeria while attending a conference.

Biographies: *Whitney M. Young Jr. and the Struggle for Civil Rights* (1989) by Nancy Weiss and *Militant Mediator* (1998) by Dennis C. Dickerson. In 2013, PBS aired the documentary *The Powerbroker: Whitney Young's Fight for Civil Rights*. A quote in reference to the documentary about him-"Whitney understood power, he understood politics, most of all he understood people. They said Martin was in the streets, Roy and Thurgood were in the courts, and Whitney was in the boardroom. One could not have been successful without the other." Vernon Jordan, CEO of National Urban League.[xlii]

And whatsoever ye shall ask in my name, that will I do, that the Father may be glorified in the Son. If ye shall ask anything in my name, I will do it. John 14:13, 14.

JAMES FARMER

Mr. Farmer was born on January 12, 1920 in Marshall, Texas. His full name is James Leonard Farmer Jr. In 1938, Farmer attended Wiley College in Marshall, Texas and Howard University in Washington, DC (1941). His father taught divinity school at Howard University.

James Farmer, one notable in the civil rights movement who helped with the sit-ins and the Freedom Riders. He was the leader and founder of CORE-Congress of Racial Equality and instrumental in the passing of the Civil Rights Acts and the Voting Right Acts. CORE was created to ensure equal rights for everyone regardless of race, creed, sex, age, disability, sexual orientation, religion or ethnic background. CORE was one of the big four civil rights organizations-NAACP, SCLC, and the SNCC.

Mr. Farmer died July 9. 1999 in Fredericksburg, Virginia. He served as assistant secretary of health, education and welfare under President Richard M. Nixon. He published his autobiography, *Lay Bare the Heart* in 1985. In 1998 he was awarded the Presidential Medal of Freedom and worked with Martin Luther King Jr. By the 1960's, he was known as "one of the Big Four" civil rights leaders in the 1960s, together with NAACP chief Roy Wilkins and Urban League head Whitney Young.[xliii]

James 1:19 Wherefore my beloved brethren, let every man be swift to hear, slow to speak, slow to wrath

HOSEA WILLIAMS

Hosea Lorenzo Williams was a civil rights leader, an ordained minister, businessman, philanthropist, scientist, and politician. He served as an officer of the SCLC during the Civil Rights Movement. Mr. Williams was born January 5, 1926 in Attapulgus, Georgia. His mother died in childbirth giving birth to his younger sister, he had to move in with his grandmother.

Hosea served in World War II in an all-black unit and received a purple heart. At age 23, Williams completed his high school education and enrolled at Morris Brown College, in Atlanta, and earned his bachelor's degree in chemistry and in the fifties earned a master's degree from Atlanta University. Williams worked as a research chemist for the US Department of Agriculture. He married Juanita Terry and became an ordained minister. They had five children together and adopted four more children.

In 1964, Hosea joined the SCLC and organized black voter registration drives. He played a major role in the March to Montgomery. This event became known as Bloody Sunday, which influenced Lyndon Johnson to sign the Voting Rights Act.

Hosea was elected to the Georgia State Assembly in 1974. He remained a representative for ten years until he resigned. His wife took over his seat. Mr. Williams was a member of the Atlanta City Council from 1985 to 1990. From 1990 to 1994 he served as DeKalb County Commissioner.

Hosea Williams died November 16, 2000. Hosea Feed the Hungry feeds thousands of people throughout the year in Atlanta, Georgia. [xliv]

Delight thyself also in the Lord, and he shall give thee the desires of thine heart. Commit thy way unto the Lord; trust also in him; and he shall bring it to pass. Psalm 37:4, 5

ROSA PARKS

Rosa Parks is known for not giving up her seat to a white patron and the mother of the Civil Rights Movement. She was born February 4, 1913, in Tuskegee, Alabama. On December 1, 1955, she refused to give her seat up to a male patron.

Quotation from Rosa Parks.

> I had problems with bus drives over the years because I didn't see fit to pay my money into the front and then go around to the back. Sometimes bus drivers wouldn't permit me to get on the bus, and I had been evicted from the bus. But as I say, there had been incidents over the years. One thing that made this get as much publicity was the fact the police were called in and I was placed under arrest. See if I had just been evicted from the bus and had not placed me under arrest or had any charges brought against me, it probably could have been just another incident. I had almost a life history of being rebellious against being mistreated because of my color.

Rosa Parks was an activist for the Scottsboro Boys. Rosa and her husband Raymond worked in the National Association for the Advancement of Colored People. She moved to Detroit in 1957. In 1964 she became a deaconess in the African Methodist Episcopal Church (AME).

Rosa wrote and published her autobiography in 1992, *Rosa Parks: My Story*. In 1995, she published *Quiet Strength*; this book is about her memoirs and her faith.

Awards and Honors

Springarn Medal given by the NAACP

Presidential Medal of Freedom given President Clinton September 9, 1996

Congressional Gold Medal 1997

Time Magazine's Twenty Most Influential People of the 20th Century-1999

A statue of her in the Capitol building by President Obama

Mrs. Parks died October 24, 2005.[xlv]

Every good and perfect gift comes from above and cometh down from the Father of lights. James 1:17

WILLIAM EDWARD BURGHARDT DUBOIS

Mr. Dubois is better known as W.E.B. DuBois, he came to earth on February 23, 1868. Mr. DuBois was a leading civil rights movement figure during the Jim Crow period. He was a very intelligent man, born in Great Barrington, Massachusetts and educated at Harvard, Fisk, and the University of Berlin.

He is author of *The Souls of Black Folk* published in 1903, a collection of fourteen essays by him. Other books by him are *The Negro* (1915), *The Philadelphia* (1899), *Black Reconstruction in America* (1935), *Writings* (1975), *Darkwater Voices from Within the Veil* (1920), *Dark Princess* (1928), *Crusaders for Peace, Worlds of Colors* and many others.

W.E.B. made contributions in various fields, sociology, history, fiction, and his own autobiography. In 1903, he left the university to find, first the Niagara Movement and then the National Association for the Advancement of Colored People. Mr. DuBois served as director of research and editor of the NAACP's *CRISIS*.

After World War II he committed himself to the cause of world peace, but as a result of that became a target of government harassment during the cold war for his alleged connections to communists. In 1961, he moved to Ghana.

Mr.DuBois died August 27, 1963.[xlvi]

God wants us to be productive and strong as the trees. The trees produce leaves and get rid of leaves. Psalms 1:3 And he shall be like a tree planted by the rivers of water that bringeth forth his fruit in his season; his leaf also shall not wither; and whatsoever he doeth shall prosper.

FANNIE LOU HAMER

Fannie Lou Hamer was born October 6, 1917 in Montgomery County, Mississippi. She was one of the hardest working women during the civil rights movement. Ms. Hamer was known for her fiery speeches at civil rights conference and was very instrumental in organizing the Mississippi Freedom Summer. It was a 1964 effort to register black voters. The struggle to get blacks registered to vote occurred because it was an effort to keep blacks powerless.

Fannie Lou worked for the Student Nonviolent Coordinating committee; it fought racial segregation and injustice in the South. Ms. Hamer, was threatened, arrested, beaten, and shot at during her civil activist adventures. As a result of the abuse, she suffered permanent kidney damage.

Ms. Hamer worked to help the poor families in need in the Mississippi County she lived in. She set up business opportunities for minorities, provided childcare services, and other family services that were needed. Fannie helped establish the National Women's Political Caucus in 1971.

Fannie died March 14, 1977. Andrew Young gave the eulogy at Hamer's funeral. He explained, "None of us would be where we are today, had she not been here then." Hundreds came to the church to say goodbye.[xlvii]

And we know that all things work together for good to them that love God. Romans 8:28

ASA PHILLIP RANDOLPH

Asa Phillip Randolph was born on April 15, 1889 in Crescent City, Florida. Mr. Randolph is the son of James and Elizabeth Randolph. Asa is the second son of the couple. His parents were supporters of equal rights for Black Americans and rights for everyone. The family moved to Jacksonville, Florida in 1891, where Asa spent his young years and he attended Cookman Institute. (now known as Bethune Cookman College).

Asa left Florida for New York to attend City College in Harlem, New York City. Mr. Randolph worked during the day and studied at night.

In the year of 1917, Mr. Randolph and his friend Chandler Owen founded the *Messenger*. It was a controversial magazine because it criticized President Woodrow Wilson, Booker T. Washington, and W.E.B. DuBois. The civil rights leaders at times had different viewpoints but knew how to come together for the movement's sake.

Mr. Randolph focus was the labor movement as it relates to the civil rights movement. One of his biggest successes in this area was the organization of the Brotherhood of Sleeping Car Porters. After hard work and determination the porters, won a contract with the railroad in 1937.

Mr. Randolph organized the 1941 March on Washington; the goal was to ban discrimination in defense industries. As a result, President Franklin D. Roosevelt issued an Executive Oder 8802 banning it. Mr. Randolph was determined; he began the development of the March on Washington in 1963 with the idea of obtaining government sponsorships of jobs for blacks. It was overshadowed by the needs of the civil rights movement in the south.

Mr. Randolph died May 16, 1979. Mr. Randolph's life has been honored through many books that have been written about his life.[xlviii]

Lamentations 3:25 The Lord is good unto them that wait for him, to the soul that seeketh him.

BOOKER T. WASHINGTON

Booker T. Washington was born in Virginia April 5, 1856, his mother Jane was a slave at this time. Jane moved to West Virginia to be with her husband. In 1881, Mr. Washington attended Hampton University and Wayland Seminary (Virginia Union University).

Mr. Washington became famous for his Atlanta address of 1895. It was called the Atlanta Compromise. He had supporters from all areas of life-ministers, educators, the community, and politicians. Mr. Washington served as an adviser to Presidents Theodore Roosevelt and William Howard Taft. Booker's views clashed with other black leaders, such as W.E.B. Dubois. Washington wrote letters that was against lynching mobs, they were written in code names.

Booker T. Washington founded the Tuskegee Institute in Alabama which is still a prominent black university. He is recognized for his educational successes and promoting economic success.

In addition, his widely read autobiography, *Up From Slavery* stands and stood as a classic.

Booker T. Washington quotes:

Associate yourself with people of good quality, for it is better to be alone than in bad company.

Nothing ever comes to one that is worth having, except as a result of hard work.

Character is power.

If you want to lift yourself up, lift up someone else.

Character, not circumstances, make the man[xlix]

Be still and know that I am God. Psalms 46:1

MEDGAR WILEY EVERS

Medgar Evers was born July 2, 1925 in Decatur, Mississippi. Mr. Evers was a civil rights activist who concentrated on overturning segregation at the University of Mississippi, social justice, and voting rights.

Medgar graduated from Alcorn University and he served in World War II. He married Myrlie Evers in 1951. Medgar Evers served as the field secretary for the NAACP; he was responsible for helping blacks gain admission to University of Mississippi, voting rights/ registration, economic justice, social justice, and public facilities. In addition, Mr. Evers investigated the lynching of Emmett Till and he was vocally supportive of Clyde Kennard, a civil rights pioneer. His works made him a prominent black leader.

Medgar was assassinated on June 21, 1963.

HONORS

1963 - Awarded the Spingarn Medal from the NAACP.

1969 Medgar Evers College established in Brooklyn, New York.

1992- Jackson, Mississippi erected a statue of him.

1992- US Highway 49 renamed in Evers honors.

2004-Jackson, Mississippi's airport was named after him. (Jackson-Medgar Wiley Evers International Airport)[1]

Proverbs 27:12 The prudent see danger and take refuge, but the simple keep going and pay the penalty.

ARTS

Do not bury your talent. There is a story in the Bible Jesus gives three people talents. Two of the people used their talents wisely. God told them he would bless them because they had been faithful over what God had given them. He said they had been faithful over a few things, and that he would give them charge of many things. Do not bury your talents or gifts that God has blessed you with. The one that was not faithful over his talent said I was afraid and hid his talent in the ground. Please do not be afraid God is with you. Do it afraid.

Exodus 31:1-6 Then the Lord said to Moses, See, I have chosen Bezalel son of Uri, the son of Hur, of the tribe of Judah, and I have filled him with the Spirit of God, with wisdom, with understanding, with knowledge and with all kinds of skills - to make artistic designs for work in gold, silver and bronze, to cut and set stones, to work in wood, and to engage in all kinds of crafts. Moreover, I have appointed Oholiab son of Ahisamak, of the tribe of Dan, to help him.

Art has been around for years, if others have created their art work; just know you can create yours. The world is in need of your gift.

MISTY COPELAND

Misty was born in Kansas City, Missouri on September 10, 1982 and was raised in San Pedro, California.

Misty Copeland is making strides as the first Black American ballet dancer breaking barriers. Misty discovered ballet dancing while she was living in a motel room with her siblings. Ms. Copeland took a free ballet class at a local Boys & Girls Club.

Ms. Copeland learned en pointe within three months and performed professional within a year. That is unheard of in the ballet arena. She began her career at thirteen. Misty attended ballet classes at San Pedro Dance Center. Cynthia Bradley the owner of the school picked her up after school because Misty's mom did not own a car.

At the early age of fifteen she won first place in the Music Center Spotlight Awards. She studied at the San Francisco Ballet School and American Ballet Theatre's Summer program on full scholarship.

In 2000, she joined American Ballet Theatre as a member of the corps de ballet. In June 2015, Misty was promoted to principal dancer, making her the first Black American woman ever to be promoted to the position in the company's seventy-five year history.

Misty has been featured in various publications and television programs, *CBS Sunday morning*, *60 minutes*, *The Today Show*,

This Week with George Stephanopoulos, MSNBC's *Melissa Harris Perry*, *Vogue*, *Essence*, *Ebony*, and *People Magazine*.

Her endorsements include American Express, Seiko, The Dannon Company, T-Mobile, COACH, and Diet Dr Pepper. Under Armour made Misty one of the faces of their "I Will What I Want" campaign with a commercial that went viral and caught 9,000,000 views.

She authored the New York Times Best-selling memoir, *Life in Motion*. It was co-written with award-winning journalist and author Charisse Jones. She authored a picture book, entitled *Firebird*. In 2014, President Obama appointed her to the President's Council on Fitness, Sports, and Nutrition.

Misty Copeland married her long-time beau Olu Evans. History is continuing, Misty has her own Barbie doll as of May 2016. The doll is part of the Barbie Sheroes program. It honors women who made it even when the odds were stacked against them and who are from diverse backgrounds. Ms. Copeland appeared on *Good Morning America* to unveil the doll.[li]

Whatever you do, work at it with all your heart, as working for the Lord, not for men, since you know that you will receive an inheritance from the Lord as a reward; it is the Lord Christ you are serving. Colossians 3:23-24 NIV

GORDON ROGER PARKS

Mr. Parks was born as Gordon Roger Alexander Buchanan Parks in Fort Scott, Kansas on November 30, 1912. Parks moved to St. Paul, Minnesota during his teenage years. When Parks graduated from high school, he was employed as a waiter, lumber-jack, piano player, band leader, and semi-professional basketball player. In 1937, he chose photography as a career. Mr. Park made Chicago his residence.

Parks won a Rosenwald Fellowship his first award for photography. Parks worked for Roy Stryker at the Farm Security Administration, he was there for a year and then went to OWI's Overseas Division and worked with Elmer Davis.

Mr. Parks reunited with Stryker in 1945 as a member of a seven man photographic team. They created documentaries for Standard Oil of New Jersey. In 1949, he was recruited by *Life* magazine as a staff photographer. While with *Life* magazine he did stories on a Harlem gang leader, segregation in the South, crime in the United States, and on the plight of an underprivileged Brazilian boy named Flavio. The A.S.M.P (American Society of Magazine Photographers) named him Magazine photographer of the Year.

In 1961, he received the Newhouse Award for photography from Syracuse University; he won honors for the Art Directors show, and won the News Pictures of the Year competition. Working as a *Life* photographer enabled him to travel the world. Parks and his family lived in Paris, France   for over a year.

Parks considers himself a weekend composer. He wrote books on photography, *The Learning Tree* published in 1963 and *A Choice of Weapons* published in 1966. Mr. Parks departed this earth on March 7, 2006.[lii]

God will give you the strength. Philippians 4:13NKJV- I can do all things through Christ who strengthens me.

CHARLES WHITE

Charles White a modern painter born April 2, 1918 in Chicago, Illinois. Mr. White married Elizabeth Catlett in 1941.

He is known for his painting 1)Move on up a Little Higher, it depicts a woman with her palms stretched heavenward; 2)Take My Mother Home, a young man has one hand raised in benediction; and 3) Mary don't you Weep, this one illustrates two women weeping. These paintings are taken straight from Christian spirituals.

Charles grew up in Chicago. He knew when he was a young boy he wanted to be an artist. His mother's window shades were his first canvases. He painted buildings and lots in his neighborhood. At the young age of fifteen he began exhibiting his work in churches, parking lots, and anywhere he could find where he captured an audience.

Mr. White attended the Art Institute of Chicago. He worked on the easel project under the Illinois Art Project WPA, and had freedom to work as he chose. A Roosevelt Fellowship, A John Hay Whitney Fellowship, and a National Institute of Arts and Letters grant was earned by him.

His work may be seen in collections in the Library of Congress, the Whitney Museum of American Art, Long Gallery in Washington, D. C., Atlanta University, Tuskegee Institute, Howard University, and the Deutsche Akademi, Berlin Germany. His work is displayed amongst private collections in France,

England, Canada, Switzerland, Italy, Africa, India, and Japan.

White received all kinds of offers to work commercially but declined. He felt he had a social responsibility. He said, "I look to life and to my people as the fountainhead of challenging ideas and monumental concepts. I look to the bright new world coming; as I face a blank canvas, it is with such thoughts that I, an American Negro, turn to the business at hand-Art."

Charles White died on October 3, 1979 in Los Angeles, California.[liii]

Our soul wait for the Lord: he is our help and our shield. Psalm 33:20.

JAMEA RICHMOND EDWARDS

Jamea Richmond-Edwards graduated Magna Cum Laude with a Bachelor of Art degree from Jackson State University in 2004 where she studied painting and drawing. She began illustrating for *The Jackson Free Press* and illustrated a children's book titled *Grandma's Biscuits* by Robert Little while in college.

Ms. Richmond earned a MFA from Howard University in 2012. Jamea is inspired by the black figures of artist Kerry James Marshall and drawings of Charles White. She offers a repertoire of portraits of black women drawn using ink and graphite. Her lionized figures are portrayed in regal poses, with eyes that possess alluring gazes and bodies adored with rich tapestries of color and patterns made of sequins, rhinestones, paper and textiles.

Richmond-Edward's work has grasped the attention of art critics including the *Washington Post* and the *Huffington Post's* "Black Artists: 30 Contemporary Art Makers under 40 You Should Know". Jamea has exhibited her artwork nationally and internationally including the Delaware Art Museum Centennial Exhibition, Wilmington, Delaware; Rush Arts Corridor Gallery, Brooklyn, NY; Parish Gallery, Washington, D.C. and Galerie Myrtis, Baltimore, Maryland. Her works are in the permanent collection of private collectors across the country, and the Embassy of the United States in Dakar Senegal. Jamea's Wings Not Meant to Fly is displayed in the living room of the Lyon's family on the television show *Empire*.[liv]

Every good and perfect gift is from above. James 1:17

NINA CHANEL ABNEY

Nina Chanel Abney was born in the year of 1982 in Harvey, Illinois.   Ms. Abney was raised by her mom, who delved in the arts, two aunts, and her grandfather. Nina interest in painting began as early as middle school. She won awards in middle school and high school and started taking art serious in high school. Nina attended Parsons School of Design.

Nina Chanel Abney finds her swift success in the art world hard to believe. "My friends say I act as if it's no big deal, but I think that's because it doesn't feel real," she says. Since graduating from Parsons in 2007, Abney has had three critically acclaimed solo exhibitions at Kravets/Wehby Gallery. She was selected for the Rubell Family Collections prestigious thirty Americans show, featuring pieces by important black artists.

Her painting *Forbidden Fruit* is on display in the Brooklyn Museum... eloping her own unique style of mixed media portraiture.[iv]

Don't give up; even ventures you have tried previously have failed. Philippians 3:13-14 Brethren forgetting those things are behind and reaching forth until those things are before. I press toward the mark for the prize of the high calling of God in Christ Jesus.

DERRICK ADAMS

Derrick Adams a young black artist born in the year of 1970 in Baltimore, Maryland. His work has sold at the Rush Philanthropic Benefit Auction, the Rhona Hoffman Gallery, the Galerie Anne De Villepoix, Goodman Gallery, in Chicago, and the Lower East Side Printshop. He has a series called The *Deconstruction Worker* it includes one hundred pieces that examine the construction of the figure and image.

Adams lives in New York and graduated from The Skowhegan School of Painting & Sculpture and The Marie Walsh Sharpe Space Program. He received a BFA from Pratt Institute and his MFA from Columbia University.

His highlights include Performa 05, Brooklyn Museum Open House, The Kitchen NYC 2010, Collette Blanchard Gallery 2010 and The Bearden Project at Studio Museum in Harlem 2011. He received the 2009 Louis Comfort Tiffany Award and an honored finalist for the 2011 William H. Johnson Prize. Derrick's art has appeared in Europe in cities such as Paris and London.

Derrick Adams stated "Sometimes you just need that." Mr. Adams made this statement referring to his exhibit *Current Club*, at the Project for Empty Space Gallery inside of New York's Penn Station.[lvi]

Have faith in God. Mark 11:22

HENRY OSSAWA TURNER

Henry Ossawa Tanner was born on June 21, 1859 in Pittsburgh, Pennsylvania.

Mr. Turner was inspired to be a painter as a small boy while watching a painter at work. Mr. Turner was thirteen years old when he watched the painter use all the colors on his easel. On that day he decided to be a painter.

Little did he know that he would face trials and tribulations facing an artist, especially a Black artist. Henry studied earnestly, his skills grew and he learned a lot about being an artist. Mr. Turner sold his first painting for forty dollars, the second one for eighty dollars, and sold a photograph for fifteen dollars, a profit was made when it was resold for two hundred fifty dollars.

The French impressionists created a stir in Europe, they encouraged people to come abroad to study. Tanner was excited and had a major exhibit in Cleveland in which he wanted to raise enough money for his trip. He sold not one painting. His talent was recognized by Bishop and Mrs. Joseph C. Hartzell. They supported him by purchasing his entire collection.

Tanner left for Rome but ended up staying in Paris. In Paris he found the perfect place to work and study. He met famous artists Benjamin Constant, who encouraged him. Tanner took a special interest in religious subjects. In 1896, his famous painting *Daniel in the Lion's Den* won him major honors. Tanner's *Resurrection of Lazarus* stunned the artistic world; it was purchased by the

French government. Honors kept coming in. He won the Salon Medal in 1897 and again in 1907. The Louisiana Purchase Prize was awarded him in 1904 and earned the Lippincott Prize in 1900. The Art Institute in Chicago awarded him the Harris Prize of five hundred in 1906.

His paintings are regarded as a combination of deep religious fervor and high artistic technique, similar to the master painters of the Renaissance.

Mr. Turner died May 25, 1937.[lvii]

And whatever you do in word or deed, do all in the name of the Lord Jesus, giving thanks through Him to God the Father. Colossians 3:17 NASB

E. SIMMS CAMPBELL

Elmer Simms Campbell was a native of St. Louis, Missouri born January 2, 1906. Elmer was the son of educators Elmer and Elizabeth Simms Campbell. Unfortunately, his father died when he was four years old. Campbell attended high school at Chicago's Englewood High School and worked as the editorial cartoonist for the school paper. He also attended the Chicago Art Institute.

No one knew that E. Simms Campbell was responsible or the artist behind a syndicated cartoon series, that appeared in *Esquire* magazine, hundreds of newspapers, and magazines. Simms created Esky, the pop-eyed mascot for Esquire. He illustrated the cartoon, *Cuties*, it was syndicated by King Features to more than one hundred forty-five newspapers. His work caught millions everywhere and it was admirable.

Mr. Campbell illustrated children books and exhibited paintings. *Esquire* spotted his talent and signed him to a long term contract. Advertising agencies sought his talent; Simms was turning out over five hundred cartoons each year.

Simms work has earned him an honor in *Current Biography*; We have Tomorrow, and Who's Who. Simms work ranked high among the top artists.

Mr. Campbell died January 27, 1971 in White Plains, New York.[lviii]

Philippians 4:6-7 Don't be anxious for anything, but in everything, by prayer and petition, with thanksgiving, present your requests to God, which transcends all understanding, will guard your hearts and your minds in Christ Jesus.

SPORTS

Sports- If you believe God has called you to be a professional athlete shoot for your dream. To be successful as an athlete you have to work hard and made sacrifices. There is a lot of training, workouts, and of course eating healthy. Everyone should work out and eat healthy but athletes have to be more focused than the average person.

God uses people to help you through your journey. Success is doing what God has called you to do. There will be hard times but the reward is great. God is no respector of persons or race.

SERENA JAMEKA WILLIAMS

Serena Williams was born September 26, 1981 in Saginaw, Michigan and she is an American professional tennis player. Experts and former tennis players regard her as the greatest female tennis player. Her parents are Richard Williams and Oracene Price. Serena's family moved to Compton, California while she was a young girl. Serena started playing tennis at the age of three. Both of her parents were her coaches in the beginning.

As of September 12, 2016, her prize money totalled $81,758,451. Her prize money will continue to rise as she continues to win.

Serena has earned the most major titles in doubles, singles, and mixed doubles. At the printing of this book she holds thirty eight major titles. This puts her fourth on the all-time list and second in the open era list.

Serena's successes

Singles:

   Her singles record is 775 wins and 129 losses.
   Australian Singles in 2003, 2005, 2007, 2009, 2010, and 2015.
   The French Open in 2002, 2013, and 2015.
   Wimbledon-2002, 2003, 2009, 2010, 2012, 2015, 2016

US Open -1999, 2002, 2008, 2012, 2013, 2014

Doubles

Her doubles career record 184 wins -30 losses

Australian Open wins 2001, 2003, 2009, 2010

French Open 1999, 2010

Wimbledon 2000, 2002, 2008, 2009, 2012, 2016

US Open 1999, 2009

Olympic Medals

2000 Sydney Gold Doubles

2008 Beijing   Gold Doubles

2012 London Gold Singles

2012 London Gold   Doubles.[lix]

To be successful in life you need wisdom. Proverbs 4:7 Wisdom is the principal thing, therefore get wisdom. And in all your getting get understanding.

VENUS WILLIAMS

Venus Ebony Starr Williams was born June 17, 1980 in Lynwood, California. She became a professional tennis player October 31, 1994. Early in her career she was coached by her father Richard Williams mainly and her mother, Oracene Price.

Venus is a strong baseliner and has a very fast serve. She is a very skilful volleyer, she uses her wingspan and she moves quickly around the net. Venus is regarded as an all-time great tennis player.

Wins in Single Tournaments

Wimbledon 2000, 2001, 2005, 2007, 2008
US Open 2000, 2001
Tour Finals 2008

Doubles

Australian Open 1999, 2010
Wimbledon 2000, 2002, 2008, 2009, 2012, 2016
US Open 1999, 2009

Olympic Medals

2000 Sydney Gold Singles
2000 Sydney Gold Doubles

2008 Beijing Gold Doubles

2012 London Gold Doubles

2016 Rio de Janeiro Silver Mixed Doubles

Venus has her own fashion line EleVen. Venus said, "I love fashion and the idea. I am using my design education to create clothing and footwear I will wear on and off the tennis court is a dream come true for me. The vision has been to create a collection that will allow women to enjoy an active lifestyle while remaining fashionable at the same time. I'm thrilled with everything we've created to launch EleVen."[ix]

Proverbs 8:1 Does not wisdom cry out, And understanding lift up her voice?

ARTHUR ASHE

Arthur was born July 10, 1943 in Richmond, Virginia. Arthur is the oldest of Arthur Ashe Sr. and Mattie Cunningham's two sons. Arthur's mother taught him how to read at the age of four. Unfortunately, his mother passed away two years later. His father put a tighter rein on his sons to make sure they stayed on the straight and narrow. Arthur and his brother Johnnie came straight home after school and went to church every Sunday.

Arthur discovered tennis a year after his mother's death. Dr. Robert Walter Johnson Jr., a tennis coach aided in Ashe's success as a tennis player.

Mr. Ashe won three grand slam titles, and was the first African American male player to win the US Open and Wimbledon. He was the first black American to be ranked number one in the world. He attended the University of California at Los Angeles. While at UCLA he was coached by J.D. Morgan and practiced very often with Pancho Gonzales, one of his mentors. Arthur graduated with a Bachelors of Business Administration. Ashe became a member of Kappa Alpha Psi fraternity and he joined the Army after graduating from college.

Ashe's community involvement consisted of creating inner city tennis programs for youth and helped create the Association of Men's Tennis Professionals. Ashe spoke against Apartheid in South Africa.

Ashe contracted the Aids Virus through a blood transfusion. He turned his efforts to raising awareness of the disease. He died on February 6, 1993. Ashe has a statue amongst Civil War generals on Monument Avenue in Richmond, Virginia. It was sculpted by Paul DiPasquale.

Quotes by Arthur Ashe

True heroism is remarkably sober, very undramatic. It is not the urge to surpass all others at whatever cost, but the urge to serve others at whatever cost.

Success is a journey not a destination. The doing is often more important than the outcome.

My father... kept me out of trouble. I had exactly twelve minutes to get home from school, and I kept to that rule through high school.[lxi]

Proverbs 29:23-A man's pride shall bring him low: But honor shall uphold the humble in spirit.

ALTHEA GIBSON

Althea Gibson was born August 25, 1937 in Silver, South Carolina. Althea played tennis with her right hand. Her parents Daniel and Annie Bell Gibson were sharecroppers on a cotton farm. The family was hit hard by the Great Depression so they moved to Harlem in the 1930's. Althea was an American tennis player, professional golfer, and was the first black athlete to cross the color lines of international tennis.

The family's domicile was an apartment in a stretch of 143rd Street that had been designated as a Police Athletic League play area. By 1939, Gibson had become proficient in paddle tennis and was New York City's women's paddle tennis champion. In 1940, a group of Gibson's neighbors took up a collection to finance a junior membership and lessons at the Cosmopolitan Tennis Club in the Sugar Hill sections of Harlem. Ms. Gibson attended Florida A & M University.

That was the beginning, in 1956; Gibson became the first African American athlete to win a Grand Slam event, the French Open singles championship, and the Wimbledon doubles championship. She won it again in 1957. Althea won the finals of eight Grand Slam events in 1957, winning the Wimbledon, US National singles titles, The Wimbledon and Australian doubles championships, the US mixed doubles crown, finished second in Australian singles, US doubles and Wimbledon mixed doubles. At seasons end she broke yet another barrier as the first black player on the US Wightman Cup team, which defeated Great Britain.

After finishing her career in tennis she played golf, sung, and acted. Ms. Gibson starred in the 1959 John Wayne film *The Horse Soldiers*; she played the role as a maid. Althea was the first black American to play for the LPGA. She was married to Sydney Llewellyn from 1983 to 1988 and Will Darbin from 1965 to 1976.

Althea Gibson died September 28, 2003.[lxii]

Proverbs 12:24- The hands of the diligent shall bear rule; but the slothful shall be under tribute.

LEROY PAIGE better known as SATCHEL PAGE

Leroy "Satchel" Paige was born July 7, 1906 in Mobile, Alabama. He received his nickname because he carried satchel bags at the train station in Mobile, Alabama. Mr. Paige was married to Janet Howard from 1934 to 1943 and Lahoma

Brown from 1947 to 1982. Satchel had several children-Lula Ouida Paige, Pamela Jean Paige, Rita Jean Paige, Linda Sue Paige, Carolyn Lahoma Paige, and Robert Leroy Paige.

He is known in the world of baseball. Satchel pitched for the Mobile Tiger, the Chattanooga Black Lookouts, and the New Orleans Black Pelicans. They paid him fifty to two hundred dollars a month.

Mr. Paige was considered a legend in the Negro League, he played in the 1948 World Series in game five between the Cleveland Indians and the Boston Braves at Cleveland. This was a milestone history making moment for him.

From 1951 to 1953 he played for the St. Louis Browns. In 1965, the Kansas City Athletes signed him for one game so he can get his pension. He pitched three innings. Paige was fifty-nine years old then. Satchel Paige was inducted into the Baseball Hall of Fame in the year of 1971.

<u>Satchel Paige Quotes:</u>

Age is a case of mind over matter. If you don't mind, it don't matter.

Work like you don't need the money. Love like you've never been hurt. Dance like nobody's watching.

Not to be cheered by praise, not to be grieved by blame, but to know thoroughly one's own virtues or powers are the characteristics of an excellent man.[lxiii]

Jesus said unto him, if thou canst believe, all things are possible to him that believeth. Mark 9:23

HANK LOUIS AARON better known as

HANK AARON

Hank Aaron was born February 5, 1934 in Mobile, Alabama. His parents were Herbert and Estella (Pritchett) Aaron. Hank has seven siblings. Aaron has a brother named Tommie who played baseball. Tommie and Hank hold the career record home runs held by a pair of siblings.

Hank signed a $200/ month contract with the Negro American League Indianapolis Clowns. Aaron was very successful, and he led the team to the 1952 Negro League World Series crown. Hank Aaron began playing with the Braves March 13, 1954. Aaron was the leader in the National League and had a batting average of.328, 200 hits, 340 total bases, and 34 doubles. He was second in the league with fourteen triples, third in slugging average .558, and third with 106 runs.

In 1957, Aaron was named the National's League Most Valuable Player. The Braves won the World Series that year. On Monday April 8, 1974, Hank Aaron hit his 715th home run, breaking Babe Ruth's record. When Aaron retired he had 755 home runs.

In 1969, he became captain of the Braves and retired after the 1976 season. Over his entire career, Aaron hit forty or more home runs eight times, had 100 or more RBIs eleven times, and a batting average of.300 or higher fourteen times. Hank set a record with twenty consecutive years of hitting at least twenty home runs.

He was inducted into the Baseball Hall of Fame in 1982. In 1990 he wrote his Autobiography, *I had a Hammer*.

Awards and Honors

April -1997 stadium named after him in Mobile, Alabama - Hank Aaron Stadium

1999- Major League Baseball created the Hank Aaron Award

2001-Hank Aaron named to MLB"S ALL CENTURY TEAM

2001 -Awarded the Presidential Citizens' Medal by President Clinton

2002-Presidential Medal of Freedom by President Bush[lxiv]

Rest in the Lord and wait patiently for him. Psalm 37:7

JACKIE ROBINSON

Jack Roosevelt "Jackie" Robinson was born January 31, 1919 in Cairo, Georgia. His parents were Jerry and Mallie Robinson, they were sharecroppers. His mother single handedly raised Jackie and her four other children.

In 1945 he played one season in the Negro Baseball league with the Kansas City Monarchs. In 1947, Brooklyn Dodgers president approached him about joining the Brooklyn Dodgers. When Jackie joined the Brooklyn Dodgers, he challenged racial segregation in the North and the South. The first year he played for the Dodgers he became the National League Rookie of the Year. He had twelve home runs, a league leading twenty-nine steals, and a batting average of .297.

In 1946 he married Rachel Isum, a nursing student he met at UCLA. They had three children, Jackie Jr., Sharon, and David. Jackie stood firmly against racial inequality. The United States Postal Service honored him with a commemorative postage stamp.

In 1949, he became the National League's Most Valuable Player of the year. He was inducted into the baseball Hall of Fame in 1962. Jackie's jersey number was forty-two and a movie about his life was produced and released in 2013.

<u>Jackie Robinson quotes:</u>

Life is not important except in the impact it has on others.

I'm not concerned with you liking or disliking me, all I ask is that you respect me as a human being.

There's not an American in this country free, until every one of us is free.

This ain't fun. But you watch me I'll get it done.[lxv]

Then Peter began to speak, "I now realize how true it is that God does not show favoritism but accepts men from every nation who fear him and do what is right. Acts 10:34-35 NIV

DEION SANDERS

Deion Sanders was born on August 9, 1967 in the city of Fort Meyers, Florida. He played baseball, basketball, football, and ran track. He was a gifted athlete and blessed with tremendous speed. In high school he won state honors in three sports (football, baseball, and basketball). Mr. Sanders attended Florida State; he was a two time All American. He won the Jim Thorpe Award in 1988 and helped the Seminoles win a Sugar Bowl victory in 1988.

Professionally Sanders was drafted and picked in the MLB draft, and the Atlanta Falcons selected him in the NFL Draft. Deion played baseball part time for the Cincinnati Reds in 1997 and played for the Braves. They won the World Series in 1992.

HONORS

Deion won all State honors in football, baseball, and basketball at North Fort Meyers High School.

Deion was elected to the Florida Sports Hall of Fame.

He was elected to the Florida State University Athletics Hall of Fame.

Eight time NFL Pro Bowler: 1991-1994 and 1996-1999.

He was a two-time Super Bowl champion 1994(San Francisco) and 1995   (Dallas).

Only player in NFL history to score a touchdown six different ways (regular and post season): kick-off return, punt return, interception return, fumbles recovery, receiving, and rushing.

Mr. Sanders stole a career high fifty six bases in 1997.

He was the only player in history to play in both the Super Bowl and World Series.[lxvi]

The Lord is good unto them that wait for him, to the soul that seeketh him. Lamentations 3:25

DOUG WILLIAMS

Doug Williams was born August 9, 1955 in Zachary, Louisiana. Williams attended Chaneyville High School and Grambling State University. He played the position of quarterback while attending the university and was very successful.

Doug was drafted to the NFL in 1978. Mr. Williams played for the Tampa Bay Buccaneers from 1978 to 1982, Arizona Outlaws in 1984, and the Washington Redskins from 1986-1989.

He was the first Black American quarterback to win a super bowl. He won the XXII Super Bowl, beating the Denver Broncos 42-10. The Redskins scored five touchdowns in the second quarter. Doug was the MVP of the Super bowl. During his tenure at the Redskins he had one hundred passing touchdowns, fifteen rushing touchdowns in eighty-eight NFL games.

His Coaching career is as follow:

Southern University 1985(Consultant), US Naval Academy (Running Backs coach) 1994, Scottish Claymores (Offensive coordinator) 1995, Jacksonville Jaguars(College Scout) 1995-1996, Morehouse College (Head Coach) 1997, Grambling State University Head Coach (1998-2003 and 2011-2013).

In 1998, Williams became the head football coach at Grambling State University. He led the Tigers to three straight years of winning the SWAC Conference from 2000-2002.

Doug's executive career in football includes Tampa Bay Buccaneers (Personnel executive) 2004-2008; Tampa Bay Buccaneers (Coordinator of pro scouting) 2009-2010; Virginia Destroyers (General Manager) 2010-2011; and Washington Redskins (Personnel executive) 2014-present.[lxvii]

The wisdom of the prudent is to understand his way: but the folly of fools is deceit. Proverbs 14:8

Walter Payton

Walter Payton was born July 25, 1953 in West Point, Mississippi. He married Connie Norwood in 1976; they gave birth to two children, Jarrett Payton and Justin Sandy. Early in life he was a member of the Boy Scouts, Little League, and his local church. Payton played drums in the marching band, ran track, and sung in the school choir. Walter attended college at Jackson State University. While at Jackson State he rushed for more than thirty-five hundred yards.

Walter Payton was a NFL nine time pro bowler. He played for the Chicago Bears thirteen years and nominated into the NFL Hall of Fame in 1993. Mr. Payton earned the nickname sweetness throughout the NFL.

His legacy includes the Walter Payton Award, The Walter Payton Man of the Year Award and a heightened awareness of the need for organ donations.

Walter won Super Bowl XX, the NFC championship in 1985, the NFL MVP, in 1976, 1977, and 1985. In 1977 and 1985, he was the offensive player of the year. The Chicago Bears retired his jersey, his number was thirty four. Throughout his career, he had 110 touchdowns and rushed 16,726 yards.

He died November 1, 1999.[lxviii]

In your purpose walk, you must, go from the presence of a foolish man, when thou perceivest not in him the lips of knowledge. Proverbs 14: 7.

DAVID MAURICE ROBINSON

David Maurice Robinson was born August 6, 1965 in Key West, Florida. He played center for the San Antonio Spurs in the National Basketball Association. Before playing basketball, he served as an admiral in the United States Navy. He earned the nickname "The Admiral."

David's family settled down in Woodbridge, Virginia after his father retired from the Navy. Robinson played basketball in high school at Osbourn Park High School in Manassas, Virginia; it's located outside of Washington DC. Robinson was an all-area and all district honors but generated little interest among college recruits. Robinson went to the United States Naval Academy, and he majored in Mathematics.

David played basketball in the Naval Academy. He chose jersey number fifty after his idol Ralph Sampson. David grew to be seven feet while in college. David was an All American basketball player, and he won the Naismith's and Woodmen Awards.

In 1986, Robinson helped the Navy win a number seven seed within a game of the Final Four before losing to Duke in the East Regional Final. In 1987, he was drafted by the San Antonio Spurs, but the Spurs had to wait two years because David had to complete his active duty obligation with the Navy.

In 1989, David was named the Rookie of the year; he came and turned the Spurs franchise around. With Robinson on the team, the Spurs went to the playoff seven seasons in a row. He won the MVP trophy in 1995. In 1996, he was named one of the fifty greatest players in the NBA history.

Awards and Honors- two time US Olympic Hall of Fame, Two-time NBA champion, 1992 Defensive player of the year, 1990 NBA rookie of the Year, 1990 NBA All – Rookie first team, Four – time All NBA First team, Four-time All- Defensive First Team, 10 time NBA all-star, 2001 NBA Sportsmanship Award, Two time Olympic Gold medal winner, Olympic bronze medal winner. Jersey Number 50 retired by the San Antonio Spurs.

Robinson is married to Valerie Hoggatt. They got married in 1991. They have three sons, David Jr. Corey, and Justin. He is a Christian.

In 2001, Robinson created the Carver Academy in San Antonio, a non-profit private school named for George Washington Carver. The school provided opportunities for inner-city children. In 2012, it became a chartered school, and the name changed to IDEA Carver. David earned his Master of Arts in Administration with a concentration in organizational development from the University of the Incarnate Word.

David Robinson partnered with Daniel Bassichis formerly of Goldman Sachs and a board member of the academy, to form the Admiral Capital Group, a private equity firm. Its goal is to invest in opportunities that can provide financial and social returns. It is designed to create financial support for the academy. The portfolio is worth 100 million it include upscale hotels, office buildings, Centerplate, Academy Sports plus Outdoors. The Admiral Capital Group partnered with Living Cities to form the Admiral Center, a non-profit created to help support other athletes and entertainers with their social initiatives. Robinson is co-owner of a Jaguar Land Rover Dealership in San Juan, Texas.[lxix]

Proverbs 13:3 He that keepeth his mouth keepeth his life: but he that openeth wide his lips shall have destruction.

GABRIELLE (GABBY) CHRISTINA VICTORIA DOUGLAS

Gabrielle Douglas was born December 31,1995 in Virginia Beach, Virginia to parents Timothy Douglas and Natalie Hawkins. Gabrielle was a member of the United States Gymnastics team at the 2012 and 2016 Summer Olympics.

In 2012, she won gold medals in both the individual all-around and team competitions. Douglas made history, by becoming the first black woman to become the individual all-around champion. In addition she was the first to win gold medals in the individual all-around and team competitions at the same Olympic. And the only all-around champion to win multiple gold medals. She was on the winning US team in the 2011 World Championship. Her nickname is Flying Squirrel.

Gabby began her training at three when her older sister Arielle, convinced their mother to enroll her in gymnastic classes. When she was fourteen, she moved from Virginia Beach to West Des Moines, Iowa to train under Liang Chow for the Olympics. Gabby sought him out as a coach after he taught her how to perform the Amanar vault in a single afternoon.

In the 2016 Olympics, Gabby helped Team USA win gold. Other medals include the AT & T American Cup All-Around Gold Medalist, and the City of Jesolo All –Around Gold Medalist. Gabby is a young lady who is determined and full of confidence.[lxx]

It's a good thing if you read the word of God. Psalm 119:105 Thy word is a lamp unto my feet, and a light unto my path.

SIMONE ARIANNE BILES

Simone Biles was born March 14, 1997 in Columbus, Ohio but currently resides in Spring, Texas. Simone's mother, Shanon Biles, was not able to take care of her and her siblings. Simone's grandfather, Ron Biles, began taking care of her in the year of 2000 along with her sister Adria. In 2003 he adopted them. His sister adopted Simone's two older siblings.

Ms. Bile's interest in gymnastics began at the age of six, soon after she enrolled at Bannon's Gymnastics and began training with coach Aimee Boorman at age eight. Ms. Biles won four gold medals in the 2016 Olympics- the vault, floor, all around, and balance beam in Rio de Janeiro. She has won world championships for three consecutive years that is 2013, 2014, and 2015. [lxxi]

Proverbs 18:2 A fool hath no delight in understanding, but that his heart may discover itself.

MUNA LEE

Muna Lee was born October 30, 1981 in Little Rock, Arkansas. She is an American Sprinter who represented the USA in the 2005 and 2008 Olympics.

Ms. Lee won a gold medal as part of the women's 4 x100m relay team at the 2005 World Championships in Athletics. She had an awesome performance in 2004 Olympic Trials and placed second to win a spot on the Olympic Team. Muna placed seventh at the Olympic Games. In the 2008 Olympics in Beijing, China she placed fifth position with a time of 11.07 seconds.

Lee ran track collegiately at Louisiana State University. Muna won the NCAA championship seven times. The SEC championship is part of her resume, she won it twelve times and she was a twenty time All-American from 2001-2004.[lxxii]

God is our refuge and strength a very present help in trouble. Psalm 46:1

JESSE OWENS

James Cleveland "Jesse" Owens was born September 12, 1913 in Oakville, Alabama, the son of a sharecropper and grandson of a slave. When Jesse turned nine, his family moved to Cleveland, Ohio. He went from a one-room schoolhouse replaced by a bigger setting. Jesse was married to Minnie Ruth Solomon from 1935-1980. They had three daughters Marlene, Beverly, and Gloria.

Jesse was a successful track star, who won four gold medals at the 1936 Berlin Olympics. He was the first Olympian to achieve this, his long jump record stood for twenty-five years. Jesse started his track and field aspirations at East Technical High School. He won three tracks and field events at the 1933 National Interscholastic Championships.

Mr. Owens knew nothing but success at the 1935 Big Ten Championships while attending Ohio State University, and earned the nickname Buckeye Bullet. Jesse tied a world record in the 100-yard dash – and set a long jump record of 26-8 ¼ that would stand for twenty-five years. He won four events at the NCAA Championships, two events at the AAU Championships and three at the Olympic trials. In 1935 Jesse competed in forty-two events winning them all.

The Germans and Adolph Hitler were expected to be the favored in the Olympics. The African Americans helped America's success at the Olympic Games in 1936. The United States won eleven gold medals, six of them by black athletes. Hitler was upset that Jesse won the 100-meter event; he stormed out of the stadium. Reports show he later congratulated Jesse. President Franklin D. Roosevelt did not meet with Owens to congratulate him. Jesse was finally recognized by Gerald Ford in 1976 with the Presidential Medal of Freedom.

After the 1936 Olympic Games, Owens retired from athletics and earned money in other ways. He competed in race car driving, horses, and played with the Harlem Globetrotters.

Jesse worked in marketing, public relations, and was an entrepreneur in Chicago, Illinois which included travel across the country speaking at conventions and business meetings. Jesse Owens, smoked cigarettes every day for most of his life. He died of lung cancer in Tucson, Arizona on March 31, 1980.[lxxiii]

Proverbs 10:4 He who has a slack hand becomes poor, but the hand of the diligent makes rich.

DEBRA (DEBBIE) THOMAS

Debra Janine Thomas was born on March 25, 1967 in Poughkeepsie, New York.

Debbie first experience or first knowledge of skating occurred when she was five. Debbie took formal lessons and winning competitions by the age of nine. Alex McGowan was her coach, and he guided her career as she trained for the Olympics.

Debra placed second in the US Novice Ladies ice skating competition. In 1983, she finished thirteenth in the Senior Ladies' Competition and won the 1983 Criterium International du Sucre in France. In 1984 she placed sixth in the National Seniors Event and second in the 1985 competition. In 1986 and 1988 she won the World Figure Skating titles and the United States championship. She was the first African American woman figure skater to be widely covered in the media in 1988 and won a bronze medal in the 1988 Winter Olympics.

Debbie graduated from Stanford University and became an orthopedic surgeon. Ms. Thomas opened up her own practice and specialized in hip replacement and knee replacement. Ms.Thomas married Vanden Hogan in 1988. Her second marriage is to Chris Bequette. They were married in 1996 and have a son Christopher Jules Bequette.

<u>Recognitions</u>

US figure Skating Hall of Fame in 2000

Served as a representative for the US Olympic Committee in 2002

Debi actively supports Make -A-Wish Foundation and Ara Parseghian Medical Research Foundation.[lxxiv]

Proverbs 10:8 A wise heart takes orders; an empty head will come unglued.

SIMONE MANUAL

Simone Manual was born August 2, 1996 in Sugarland, Texas. Simon attended Fort Bend Austine High School. She has two brothers who encouraged her to swim. Simone is a freestyle swimmer and swims for Stanford University.

Simone Manuel won a total of four medals at the 2016 Olympics in Rio De Janeiro. Ms. Manuel won a silver in the women's 50 meter freestyle, silver in the 4x100 freestyle relay, gold with her 100 freestyle, and gold with her freestyle leg 4x100 meter medley relay. She has won world championships in Barcelona, Spain and Kazan Tatarsan, Russia.[lxxv]

Proverbs 4:23 Keep thy heart with all diligence, For out of it are the issues of life.

POLITICS

Politics-Someone has to be the president, vice president, senators, representatives, judges, sheriffs, and other positions. Politicians are elected to represent the people.

You have to be a tough person because your character and integrity is always on the line. A true leader walks in integrity. You may not be popular but the question is who you have to answer to in the end. Just ask God to help you. He will lead and guide you every step of the way.

Politicians are governments under God. Everyone is called to do the right thing that includes politicians, congress, judges, sheriffs, etc. Romans 13:1, 2 Be a good citizen. All governments are under God. Insofar as there is peace and order, it's God's order. So live responsibly as a citizen. If you're responsible to the state, then you're irresponsible with God, and God will hold you responsible.

Proverbs 3:5, 6 Trust in the Lord with all your heart and lean not on your own understanding; in all your ways submit to him, and he will make your paths straight.

PRESIDENT OBAMA

Barack Hussein Obama II was born on August 4, 1961 in Honolulu, Hawaii. When he was a youth his nickname was Barry.

Barack's parents are Barack Obama Sr. and Ann Dunham. Barack Married Michelle Robinson in 1992. They have two children Malia Ann Obama and Sasha Obama.

Obama wrote: "The opportunity that Hawaii offered-to experience a variety of cultures in a climate of mutual respect-became an integral part of my world view, and a basis for the values that I hold most dear."

After high school, Obama moved to Los Angeles in 1979 to attend Occidental College. Obama made his first public speech, asking for Occidental to participate in the disinvestment from South Africa to respond to that nation's policy of Apartheid. When he became a junior, he transferred to Columbia University in New York City. He majored in political science with a specialty in international relations.

President Obama is the first president born in Hawaii, and the first Black American to be elected as the President of the United States not once but twice (elected in 2008 and 2012).

Accomplishments

June 1985 to May 1988- Community Organizer /Director of the Developing Communities Project. It was a church based community organization.

Fall of 1988- Entered Harvard Law /School

1991- He graduated from Harvard with a JD degree magna cum laude.

1995- Manuscript for book was published –*Dreams from My Father*.

1991- Accepted a two year position as Visiting Law and Government /Fellow at the University of Chicago Law School

1992 to 1996-Taught constitutional law at the University of Chicago Law School

1996 to 2004- Senior Lecturer Taught constitutional law at the University of Chicago Law School.

2004- Elected to the Illinois Senate in November

2007- Began his presidential campaign.

2008- Became the presidential nominee for the Democratic Party.

2008- Won the presidential nomination in the general election by defeating John McCain.

2009- He was inaugurated as the president on January 2009.

2009- Named the Nobel Peace prize laureate.

2010 -Economic stimulus signed into legislature – Tax Relief, Unemployment Insurance Reauthorization, Job Creation Act, Patient Protection and Affordable Care Act (Obama care), Dodd-Frank Wall Street Reform and Consumer Protection Act, Don't Ask, Don't Tell Repeal Act of 2010. He ended Military Involvement in the Iraq War.

2011- Budget Control Act of 2011

2012 -American Taxpayer Relief Act of 2012

2012 -Obama Re-elected president in November 2012

2013- Sworn in for a second term on January 20, 2013

2013- Signed 23 executive orders for gun control on January 16, 2013

2014- Recommended the FCC reclassify Internet service as a telecommunication service to preserve net neutrality. Negotiated a restoration of relations with Cuba after nearly sixty years of detente.

Plus much more.

Quotes:

Money is not the only answer, but it makes a difference.

If you're walking down the right path and you're willing to keep walking, eventually you'll make progress.

The future rewards those who press on. I don't have time to feel sorry for myself. I don't have time to complain. I'm going to press on.

Change will not come if we wait for some other person or some other time. We are the ones we've been waiting for. We are the change that we seek.[lxxvi]

Psalm 62: 5 My soul wait thou only upon God.

FIRST LADY MICHELLE OBAMA—MICHELLE LAVAUGHN ROBINSON

Michelle Lavaughn Robinson Obama, the first Black American first lady, was born January 17, 1964 in Chicago, Illinois. Her parents are Marian Shields Robinson and Fraser C. Robinson III. Michelle attended Whitney Young High School, Chicago's first magnet high school and Princeton University. She graduated cum laude with a Bachelor of Arts degree in 1985. Mrs. Obama studied at Harvard Law School in 1988 and worked for the Harvard Legal Aid Bureau, which assisted low-income tenants with housing problems.

Our first lady met Barack when they worked for a law firm; she mentored him when he was a summer associate. Michelle and Barack married in October 1992 and have two daughters Malia Ann and Sasha.

Mrs. Obama worked for Chicago City Hall as assistant commissioner of planning and development and the University of Chicago, as Associate Dean of Student Services.

Michelle is known for her Let's Move campaign. During the month of January 2010, she took her first lead role in an administrative-wide initiative to reverse the childhood obesity epidemic with The Let's Move campaign. This movement involves community leaders, educators, medical professionals, and parents.

She created an organic garden at the White House and wrote a book entitled 2012 book *American Grown: The Story of the White House Kitchen Garden and Gardens Across America*.

Mrs. Michelle Obama was named as *Essence* "25 of the World's Most Inspiring Women." *Vanity Fair* listed her among "10 of the World's Best Dressed People."

Since becoming our first lady, she has been an advocate for education for adolescent girls all over the world; her initiative is entitled "Let Girls Learn." Her heartfelt concerns have been taken to Broadway, *Broadway Shines a Light on Girls Education*. She is very inspiring; she created a video rap encouraging high school students to go to college.

In 2011, Michelle Obama founded Joining Forces to support service men, veterans, and their families. The goal is to make ensure veterans and their families have wellness, education, and employment opportunities. In 2014, she developed Reach Higher to encourage young people across America to get an education past high school. It can be a university, trade school, community college, or a professional training program.

Part of her farewell speech from the White House, *If your family doesn't have much money, I want you to remember that in this country, plenty of folks, including me and my husband we started out with very little. With a lot of hard work and a good education, anything is possible, even becoming president. That's what the American dream is all about.*"[lxxvii]

Let love and faithfulness never leave you; bind them around your neck, write them on the tablet of your heart. Then you will win favor and a good name in the sight of God and man. Proverbs 3:3-4.

ERNEST GREEN

Ernest Gideon Green was born September 22, 1941 in Little Rock, Arkansas. Mr. Green's parents are Lothaire and Ernest Green Sr. His mother was a member of the NAACP; she took part in protests against unequal pay between blacks and whites.

Ernest became one of the Little Rock Central High Nine because his parents decided to become plaintiffs in the lawsuit that desegregated the famous Central High School. The Central High Nine is a group Black students who integrated the school in 1957. The nine students had resistance; they were verbally abuse and received threats daily. The National Guard was called in to escort them to their classes. Ernest was the only senior of the group.

After Ernest Green Jr. graduated from high school he attended Michigan State University. Ernest Jr. was a beneficiary of a scholarship the donor was anonymous.

During his time at the university he became a charter member of Omega Psi Phi and he engaged in supporting The Civil Rights movement. He received a Bachelor of Arts in 1963 and a Master's degree in sociology in 1964. Green was successful at the university; he was in the top of his class. He married Phyllis Green and they have three children MacKenzie Green, Adam Green, and Jessica Green.

Ernest worked at a non-profit organization, the A. Phillip Randolph Education Fund from 1968-1977. He gained experience in government by becoming the Assistant Secretary of Housing and Urban Affairs under President Jimmy Carter (1977-1981). Green and Herman, consulting firm hired him as a partner in 1981. In 1985, Ernest became managing director of Lehman Brothers. Green has been portrayed in two made for television movies about the Central High Nine, *Crisis at Central High*, and the *Ernest Green Story*.[lxxviii]

In all labor there is profit: but the talk of the lips tendeth only to penury. Proverbs 14:23.

OSCAR DEPRIEST

Oscar DePriest was born March 9, 1871 in Florence, Alabama. Oscar's mother was Martha Karsner, she worked part-time as a laundress and Neander DePriest his father was a teamster, which was part of the Exodus movement (black emigration to western territories).

In 1878, his family moved to Dayton, Ohio because of the racial violence in Alabama.

Mr. DePriest married Jessie L. Williams in 1873. They had two sons Laurence W. DePriest and Oscar Stanton DePriest Jr.

In 1928, he became the first African American elected to the House of Representatives in the twentieth century. He was elected to Illinois's 1st Congressional District making him the first African American elected to the House from the North (1929 to 1935). DePriest used his position to fight for African Americans.

Mr. DePriest was very instrumental in the passage of the amendment to eliminate racial discrimination in the Civilian Conservation Corps. He defied southern racism by speaking in the South, despite threats on his life, and challenged Senator James Heflin of Alabama by eating in the Senate restaurant.

There is an Oscar DePriest House, a National Historic Landmark in Chicago, Illinois. It is located at 45th and King Drive.

Oscar died May 12, 1951.[lxxix]

Proverbs 15:1 A soft answer turneth away wrath: but grievous words stir up anger.

MARY MCCLEOD BETHUNE

Mary McCleod Bethune was born July 10, 1875 in Mayesville, South Carolina. Samuel and Patsy McLeod her parents, were former slaves and so were her brothers and sisters. Ms. MeCleod's parents had seventeen children, she was number fifteen. Mary showed leadership qualities at an early age, she walked five miles to school every day. After she made it home every day she taught the rest of the family.

The Florida East Coast grew due to the construction of the railroad. Bethune knew that education would be very important. Her interest in education became evident when she rented a two-story house in Daytona Beach, Florida and established a school for young black girls. The school had six pupils, five girls and her son. It was hard initially, she did the teaching, administrative duties, handling the money, and kept the school clean.

In 1912, the school grew, and was able to interest James M. Gamble of Procter and Gamble to become a contributor and serve as chairman of its board of trustees until he died. In the year of 1923, the school for girls merged with Cookman Institute of Jacksonville, Florida, a school for boys. The first name of the school was Bethune-Cookman Collegiate Institute, later renamed Bethune-Cookman College.

Ms. Bethune founded and was the president of the National Council of Negro Women. By 1955, the organization had a membership of eight hundred thousand. In addition she was a member of President Franklin Delano Roosevelt's "Black Cabinet" of advisers on racial matters in the year of 1932. President Roosevelt appointed her director of African American affairs in the National Youth Administration and a special adviser on minority affairs. From 1939-1945, she served as special assistant to the secretary of war during World War II. Ms. Bethune had many government assignments, honorary degrees, and awards.

Mary was one of the American observers who attended the 1945 conference in San Francisco to establish the United Nations.

Ms. Bethune died May 18, 1955 in Daytona Beach, Florida. [lxxx]

Proverbs 15:10 Message Bible It's a school of hard knocks for those who leave God's path, a dead-end street for those who hate God's rules.

BARBARA JORDAN

Barbara Jordan was born February 21, 1936 in Houston, Texas.

Ms. Jordan graduated from Texas Southern University in 1956 and continued her studies at Boston University Law School. After graduating she returned to Texas and established her law practice.

Ms. Jordan, the first black woman to win an election to a state office position and became a Texas state senator in 1966. She served in the House of Representatives in Washington DC from 1972 to 1978. One notable accomplishment was she created the Texas Fair Employment Practices Commission.

Other accomplishments:

Barbara was recognized nationally with her speech on the House floor recommending impeaching President Richard Nixon and served on the House Judiciary Committee.

In 1976 at the Democratic National Convention she spoke with excellent political oration.

Jordan gave an awesome speech at the Democratic National Convention in the year of 1992.

In 1994, she headed the Commission on Immigration Reform in America. President Bill Clinton asked her to serve.

Barbara Jordan died January   17, 1996.[lxxxi]

Proverbs 15:19 (The Message Bible) The path of lazy people is overgrown with briers; the diligent walk down a smooth road.

SHIRLEY CHISHOLM

Shirley Anita St. Hill Chisholm was born November 30, 1924 in Brooklyn, New York. Ms. Hill graduated from Brooklyn College in 1946, afterwards she was employed as a teacher. Shirley decided to continue her education by earning a master's degree in elementary education from Columbia University.

From 1953 to 1959, Chisolm served as director of the Hamilton-Madison Child Care Center and an educational consultant for New York City's Bureau of Child Welfare from 1959 to 1964.

Mrs. Chisholm was a politician, educator, and an author. In 1968 she became the first African American woman elected to Congress; she represented New York's 12th District for seven terms until 1983. In the year of 1969, Chisholm was one of the founders of the Congressional Black Caucus.

During her tenure in Congress, she was a champion in minority education and employment opportunities.

On January 23, 1972, she received 162 delegates for the nomination of the President of the United States. The closest any woman had become.

Shirley Chisholm has been spotlighted in PBS's *The Contenders: 16 for 16 Premiere*. Mrs. Chisholm had a passion for politics and did not mind shaking things up with a straight forward approach. When she ran for the presidential office she had an unbossed and unbought attitude which enabled her to receive the delegates mentioned   above.

Shirley Chisholm quotes:

Tremendous amounts of talent are lost to our society just because that talent wears a skirt.

Congress seems drugged and inert most of the time… its idea of meeting a problem is to hold hearings or, in extreme cases, to appoint a commission.

You don't make progress by standing on the sidelines, whimpering and complaining. You make progress by implementing ideas.

Ms. Chisholm died on January 1, 2005. [lxxxii]

Proverbs 15: 22 (The Message Bible) Refuse good advice and watch your plans fail; take good counsel and watch them succeed.

JOHN LEWIS

John Robert Lewis was born February 21, 1940 in Troy, Alabama. Representative Lewis was married to Lillian Miles from 1968 to 2012, until her death. They had one son John Miles Lewis. He is a civil rights movement icon that marched with Martin Luther King on bloody Sunday. When John was young, he committed to getting a quality education for himself. John was inspired by Rosa Parks and Dr. Martin Luther King.

Mr. Lewis graduated from the American Baptist Theological Seminary in Nashville, Tennessee and received a Bachelor's degree in Religion and Philosophy at Fisk University. Lewis and his fellow students sat at lunch counters to desegregate them. They were harassed, spit upon, beaten, finally arrested, and held in jail. In 1961, Lewis joined fellow students on the Freedom Rides, challenging the segregation of interstate buses.

Lewis founded the Student Nonviolent Coordinating Committee (SNCC). He served as the president from 1963 to 1966. This organization was formed as the student movement for Civil Rights. In 1963, he was known as one of the Big Six leaders of the Civil Rights movement along with Dr. King, Whitney Young, A Phillip Randolph, James Farmer, and Roy Wilkins. In 1964, Lewis was responsible for registering black voters.

On March 7, 1965, this is known as "Bloody Sunday", Lewis and fellow activist Hosea Williams led over 600 marchers across the Edmund Pettus Bridge in Selma, Alabama. Alabama State Troopers met them at the end of the bridge and ordered them to leave. The marchers refused to leave. The troopers sent tear gas and beat them with night sticks. Lewis's skull was fractured; he escaped to a church for shelter. John Lewis appeared before the television cameras calling on President Johnson to intervene in Alabama.

Lewis settled in Atlanta, Georgia, President Jimmy Carter asked him to head the federal volunteer agency, ACTION. In 1981, John Lewis was elected to the Atlanta City Council, and was an effective advocate of neighborhood preservation and government reform. In 1986, he ran for Congress and elected to the United States House of Representatives.

Congressman Lewis has received numerous honorary degrees and awards, including the 1) Martin Luther King, Jr. Non-Violent Peace Prize, 2) the NAACP Spingarn Medal, 3)The Martin Luther King Jr. Memorial Award of the National Education Association, and

4) The John F. Kennedy "Profile in Courage" award for lifetime achievement. John Lewis authored *Walking with the Wind: A Memoir of the Movement*, published in 1998.

Rep. Lewis quoted August 5, 2016, "On August 6, 1965—Fifty one years ago--*I was looking over the shoulder of President Lyndon Johnson as he signed the Voting Rights Act (VRA) of 1965 into law. It was a crowning moment in the struggle for human dignity in this country that opened access to the ballot box for millions of Americans.*" [lxxxiii]

But without faith it is impossible to please him, for he that cometh to God must believe that he is, and that he is a rewarder of them that diligently seek him.

JESSE JACKSON

Reverend Jesse Louis Jackson Sr. was born October 8, 1941 in Greenville, South Carolina.

He married Jacqueline Brown in 1962.

Jesse Jackson is a Baptist Minister, politician, and civil rights activist. He worked with Martin Luther King during the Selma to Montgomery marches. King gave Jackson a role in the Southern Christian Leadership Conference (SCLC).

Rev. Jackson founded Rainbow /PUSH. It stands for People United to Save Humanity (Operation PUSH) officially began operations on December 25, 1971. Jackson later changed the name to People United to Serve Humanity. The goal of PUSH was towards politics and to influence politics to work to improve economic opportunities for blacks and poor people of all races.

Jackson's influences extend to international matters. Reverend Jackson travelled to Syria to secure the release of a captured American pilot, Navy Lit. Robert Goodman. During the Persian Gulf War, Jackson made a trip to Iraq, to plead Saddam Hussein for the release of foreign nationals held as human shields. He has been successful in other foreign endeavors.

In the year of 2015, he called on lawmakers to discuss officer involved shootings in Chicago at a White House conference. Per Rev. Jackson the Republicans and Democrats remain silent about the Chicago violence.[lxxxiv]

Do not be deceived: God cannot be mocked. A man reaps what he sows. Those who sows to please his sinful nature, from that nature will reap destruction; the one who sows to please the Spirit will reap eternal life. Galatians 6:7-8

ENTREPRENEURS

United States need all types of business people to keep the economy growing. It can be a small, medium, or large business. Some people can design clothes, style hair, work on cars, repair homes, do taxes, sell stocks/ bonds, own your construction company, engineering company, have your own veterinary practice and the list goes on and on. Prepare for it and go for it.

There were entrepreneurs in the Bible, Lydia was one of them, and she was a dealer of purple. In Acts 16:14 Lydia was listening to Paul's message --One of those listening was a woman from the city of Thyatira named Lydia, a dealer in purple cloth.

Nehemiah 13: 15,16 In those days I saw people in Judah treading winepresses on the Sabbath and bringing in grain and loading it on donkeys, together with wine, grapes, figs, and all other kinds of loads. And they were bringing all this into Jerusalem on the Sabbath. People from Tyre who lived in Jerusalem were bringing in fish and all kinds of merchandise and selling them in Jerusalem on the Sabbath to the people of Judah.

As you see entrepreneurs were serious in biblical days about selling their goods. I say to you be bold be strong in the Lord. Go ahead and create history. And remember age is just a number it is never too late to start a business.

Let the entrepreneurs below encourage and inspire you.

FARRAH GRAY

Farrah Gray was born September 9, 1984. Mr. Gray grew up on Chicago's South side. His father is Khalid Abdul Muhammad, who was a black activist.

At age twenty, Gray may be one of the youngest millionaires in the world. He grew up in Chicago and had experienced poverty and many other social hardships during his childhood. Mr. Gray started his first business at age six by selling household objects. When Gray was thirteen, he managed to convince a group of businessmen to invest in his venture and he then started his first company: FarrOut Foods.

Farrah Gray is undoubtedly one of the most inspiring young black entrepreneurs. He received an Honorary Doctorate degree in Humane Letters from Allen University.

Farrah Gray has inspired millions all over the country. He has appeared on *Starting Over*, *20/20*, *Good Morning America*, *ABC World News Tonight*, *Oprah & Friends*, *Tom Joyner Show*, *The Michael Baisden Show*, *The Tavis Smiley Show*, *BET*, *BRAVO*, *PBS*, *NPR*, *Bloomberg*, *Essence*, *Washington Post*, *The Wall Street Journal*, and the *New York Post*.

At eight, Gray became co-founder of Urban Neighborhood Enterprise Economic Club (U.N.E.E.C.) on Chicago's South side. U.N.E.E.C. is the forerunner of New Early Entrepreneur Wonders (NE2W), the flagship organization he opened on Wall Street. The organization enlisted, educated and engaged "at-risk" youth by creating and developing legal ways for them to acquire additional income. He is the youngest person to have an office on Wall Street.

Farrah is a co-host of *Backstage Live* a syndicated television and radio simulcast in Las Vegas. The Farrah Gray Foundation focuses on inner city community based entrepreneurship education and provides scholarship and grant assistance for students from at risk backgrounds to attend HBCU's (Historically Black Colleges and Universities). Farrah has so many accomplishments; including being an author of *Get Real, Get Rich, Reallionaire: Nine Steps to Becoming Rich from the Inside Out*, and *The Truth Shall Make You Rich*.

"Quotes by Farrah":

Do not let the behavior of others destroy your inner peace.

A female that remains loyal to you without a relationship is a female you should wife.

Be picky with who you invest your time in, wasted time is worse than wasted money.

Money doesn't change you it just magnifies who you really are.[lxxxv]

God is faithful, by whom ye were called unto the fellowship of his Son Jesus Christ our Lord. I Corinthians 1:8.

SHELTON JACKSON (SPIKE) LEE

Spike Lee is the owner of 40 Acres and a Mule Filmworks. His film company has produced over thirty five films. Spike Lee was born in Atlanta, Georgia on March 20, 1957. He left Atlanta at an early age and moved to Brooklyn, New York.

Spike married Tonya Lewis. They have two children Jackson Lee and Satchel Lee. His parents are Bill and Jacquelyn Lee. Bill was a jazz musician and his mother a school teacher.

Lee attended Morehouse College and studied film at Clark Atlanta University. He also attended the Tisch School of Arts graduate film program. His first production was a short film *The Answer* (1980), a reworking of D.W. Griffith's *The Birth of a Nation.* (1915). After that Spike produced Joe's Bed-Stuy *Barbershop: We Cut Heads* (1983). It won a student Academy Award.

In 1986, he produced *She's Gotta Have It*, this production cost him $175,000, and it earned him $7 million at the box office. As a result of this success he started 40 Acres and a Mule.

Mr. Lee produced *School Daze* in 1988 and *Do the Right Thing* in 1989. Denzel Washington began acting in his movies in 1990 and they are *Mo' Better Blues*, *Malcom X* in 1992, *He Got Game* 1998, and *Inside Man* in 2006. Denzel won an Oscar Nomination for *Malcom X*.

Spike is a documentarian and he earned a Peabody Award for his biography of Black Panther leader, Huey Newton, *A Huey*

Newton Story in 2001. He won an Emmy in 2005 for his post examination of *Katrina, When the Levees Broke: A Requiem in Four Acts* and its follow up five years later, *If God is Willing and da Creek Don't Rise* (2010).

Spike Lee and his production company create independent films for major studios, he has internships for aspiring filmmakers, and he works in the community, and releases music.[lxxxvi]

And my God will meet all your needs according to his glorious riches in Christ Jesus. Philippians 4:19

TYLER PERRY

Tyler Perry was born September 14, 1969, he was raised in New Orleans by Willie Maxine (Campbell) and Emmitt Perry. He is the founder and President of Tyler Perry Company, Perry had experienced extreme poverty before he became one of the most successful producers.

In the year of 1991, he was working on a job, when he saw an episode of *The Oprah Winfrey Show* (1986) which was about the healing nature of writing. This episode inspired him to begin writing and began writing letters to himself. Tyler wrote about his bad experiences, these letters started his career. He turned his letters into plays. His first play was *I know I've Changed*.

Perry became famous in 2005 after the release of his production *Diary of a Mad Black Woman*. He has written a book and created a comedy series called The *House of Payne*. Tyler Perry wrote and produced many stage plays in the 1990s. He has opened his own studio in metro Atlanta in 2006 and moved into the current facilities in the fall of 2008.

His TV shows are *Meet the Browns, The Have and the Have Nots, Love thy Neighbor, Too Close to Home*, and *For Better or Worse*. He has several movies to his credit: *Why Did I Get Married, Why Did I Married Too, Madea's Family Reunion, Alex Cross, I Can Do Bad All By Myself, Diary of a Mad Black Woman, The Family That Preys, Temptations, Good Deeds, Single Mom's Club, Daddy's Little Girls*, and host of movies with

Madea in them. Tyler Perry is very successful as a writer, director, and producer of stage, television, and film.[lxxxvii]

A man that hath friends must shew himself friendly: and there is a friend that sticketh closer than a brother. Proverbs 18:24

EARVIN (MAGIC) JOHNSON JR.

Magic Johnson is a successful entrepreneur, and he was a very successful basketball player. Magic Johnson Enterprises serves communities and promotes economic empowerment. The business builds businesses and helps them grow. The enterprise concentrates in the areas of food, entertainment, sports, and staffing.

Magic Johnson was born August 14, 1959 in Lansing, Michigan. His parents are Earvin Sr. and Christine. His father worked at General Motors as an assembly worker and his mother was a school custodian. Johnson has six siblings.

Magic played basketball in junior high and high school. He was very good at it, he attended Michigan State, and they won an NCAA Championship during his time there. Magic played for the Los Angeles Lakers, he won five championships and received NBA Finals Most Valuable Player Award in his rookie season.

Johnson was a member of the 1992 United States Men's Olympic Team. Magic is one of seven players who have received an NCAA Championship, an NBA Championship, and an Olympic Gold Medal.

Magic announced in 1991 that he was HIV positive. Since then he has been an advocate, and he speaks for HIV/AIDS prevention and safe sex. Ebony Magazine named him as one of the most influential businessmen in 2009. Magic was part owner of the Lakers for some years. He is part of a group of investors that purchased the Los Angeles Dodgers in 2012 and the Los Angeles Sparks in 2014.

Magic Johnson launched Aspire TV Network on June 27, 2012. It's owned by Magic Johnson Enterprises. The slogan is Our Past, Our Now, Our Next, and That's Aspire. It's headquartered in Atlanta, Georgia.[lxxxviii]

Let your conversation be without covetousness; and be content with such things as ye have: for he hath said, I will never leave thee, nor forsake thee. Hebrews 13:5

MADAME WALKER

Sarah Breedlove McWilliams Walker better known as Madame Walker, together with Marjorie Joyner improved the hair care and cosmetics industry early in the 20th century.

Madame Walker was born in 1867 in poverty-stricken rural Louisiana. Walker was the daughter of former slaves, orphaned at the age of seven and widowed by twenty.

After her husband's death, the young widow migrated to St. Louis, Missouri, seeking opportunities and a better way of life for herself and her child. She supplemented her income as a wash woman by marketing and selling her homemade beauty products door-to-door. Eventually, Walker's products formed the basis of a thriving national corporation employing at one point over 3,000 people. That was a lot of people during those times.

Her Walker System, which included a broad offering of cosmetics, licensed Walker Agents, and Walker Schools, offered meaningful employment and personal growth to thousands of Black women. Madame Walker's aggressive marketing strategy combined with relentless ambition led her to be labelled as the first known African-American woman to become a self-made millionaire.

An employee of Madame Walker's empire, Marjorie Joyner, invented a permanent wave machine. This device, patented in 1928, curled or "permed" women's hair for a relatively lengthy period. The wave machine was popular and was known for creating longer lasting wavy hair styles. Joyner went on to become a prominent figure in Madame Walker's industry, though she never profited directly from her invention, for it was the assigned property of the Walker Company.[lxxxix]

God is no respecter of persons. He loves all races. What he has done for others he will do for you.

MELLODY HOBSON

Mellody Hobson was born April 3, 1969, in Chicago Illinois. She is the youngest of six kids and the first and only sibling to graduate from college, she attended Princeton University.

Mellody is an American businesswoman and the president of Ariel Investments and previously served on the Board of Directors of DreamWorks Animation. Ariel Investments is a Chicago based investment management firm. Ms. Hobson became the president in 2000.

In the mid-1990s, Mellody the founder of Ariel Investments founded Ariel Community Academy, a public school on the South Side of Chicago that includes course work on financial literacy. The children that attend the academy know more about the stock market than their parents. Mellody has served as the director of Groupon Inc. and Starbucks Corporation.

Hobson acknowledges that talking about race is "like touching the third rail," but argues that it's necessary to foster change. There is a quantifiable difference in opportunity for people of color. Hobson says and avoiding talking about it is holding back our businesses and our economy. Diversity is essential for creative problem-solving."

"We cannot afford to be color blind," she says, 'we have to be color brave. Not because it's the right thing to do, but because it's the smart thing to do."[xc]

Therefore if any man be in Christ, he is a new creature, old things are passed away, behold all things are become new. II Corinthians 5:17

NICOLE LYONS

Nicole Lyons is a race car driver who has followed in her father's footsteps as a race car driver in Los Angeles, California. She is the first Black female American race car driver.

Nicole is committed to racing and is responsible for building awarding winning engines. Cole Muscle Cars (CMC), a business Ms. Lyons started, operates in Los Angeles and Atlanta. It specializes in anything a custom car needs, Bentleys, race cars, engines, custom interior, body paint, suspension, plus much more.

Ms. Lyons went from NHRA to NASCAR IN THE YEAR OF 2013. She competed in the NASCAR Whelen Series finishing in the Top 10. Her sponsors were Royal Purple, Bell Helmets, and Pacific Equipment.

Nicole has appeared on Fox TV show *Car Warriors*. The appearances on this show landed her the 2013 Obama Leadership Award and she won the 2013 Georgia Entertainment Award for "People to Watch".

In 2014, Nicole moved up from the NASCAR Whelen Series to racing in the NASCAR KN Series driving for MAX Siegle and Rev Racing.

Her father Jack Davis taught her the culture of drag racing, how to work a wrench, and how to drive a fast car. Her father passed in 2005. Lyons said: "I think my father would be proud. He taught me what I know today about racing. He taught me that you can't be just the driver that gets in the car and drives. You need to know what the car is doing. You need to know the engine set up. My advantage is that by knowing my car, I can make good decisions out there on the track where it counts."[xci]

But it is good for me to draw near to God; I have put my trust in the Lord God, that I may declare all thy works. Psalms 73:28

MUSICIANS

Music is relaxing, encouraging, and a stress reliever. We dance to music and listen to it as we eat and drive. It can be very soothing to your soul. There are jazz, neo soul, blues, country/western, hard rock, soft rock, Latino, and gospel musicians. People have their choice of which genre they like. Music has been around for ages. Musicians dates back to biblical days.

The earth is the Lord and the fullness thereof. God created music. Lucifer was an angel in heaven in charge of praise and worship. He became full of himself and was thrown out of heaven.

The trumpeters and musicians joined in unison to give praise, and thanks to the Lord. Accompanied by trumpets, cymbals and other instruments, the singers raised their voices in praise to the Lord and sing. "He is good his love endures forever."

Psalm 68:25 In front are the singers, after them the musicians, with them are the young women playing the timbrels.

Some people are so gifted that you play your instruments by ear. That is a blessing,

If it's your desire to play your instrument, I pray that you are brave enough to do it.

The list of musicians in this section is designed to educate, remind, and inspire you.

DUKE ELLINGTON

Duke Ellington was born Edward Kennedy "Duke" Ellington. He was known for his Cotton Club orchestra appearances in Harlem. Duke was an American composer, pianist, and bandleader. Duke wrote more than one thousand compositions. Duke was awarded a special Pulitzer Prize for music in 1999.

He was born April 29, 1899 to James Edward Ellington and Daisy (Kennedy) Ellington in Washington DC. Both of his parents were pianists. Duke began playing the piano at the age of eleven.

Ellington produced eight records in 1924. Despite his advancing age (he turned 65 in the spring of 1964), Ellington showed no sign of slowing down as he continued to make vital and innovative recordings, including *The Far East Suite* (1966*), New Orleans Suite* (1970), *Latin American Suite* (1972) and *The Afro-Eurasian Eclipse* (1971), much of it inspired by his world tours. It was during this time that he recorded his only album with Frank Sinatra, entitled *Francis A. & Edward K* (1967).

Although he made two more stage appearances before his death, Ellington performed what is considered his final full concert in a ballroom at Northern Illinois University on March 20, 1974.

Following Duke's death, his son Mercer took over leadership of the orchestra, continuing until his own death in 1996. Like the Count Basie Orchestra, this group continued to release albums long after Duke Ellington's death. *Digital Duke*, credited to The Duke Ellington Orchestra, won the 1988 Grammy Award for Best Large Jazz Ensemble Album. Mercer's children continue a connection with their grandfather's work.[xcii]

Proverbs 24: 1, 2 - Be not thou envious against evil men, neither desired to be with them. For their heart studieth destruction, and their lips talk of mischief.

KIRK WHALUM

Kirk was born in Memphis, Tennessee on July 11, 1958. Mr. Whalum married his wife Ruby in 1980. They have one child, Kyle Whalum.

Kirk attended Melrose High school and Texas Southern University. He performed in the Ocean of Soul Marching Band at Texas Southern University. Kirk sung in his father's church choir. He learned to love music through his grandmother and is influenced by gospel, rock, and jazz. His emphasis is on melody, he loves the melody. While living in Houston, he was a regular at local jazz clubs.

Kirk performed at Jean Michel Jarre's concerts - Rendez-Vous Houston and Rendez-vous Lyon. He performed the song "Ron's Piece," a song dedicated to Ron McNair, who died in the Challenger disaster.

Kirk has collaborated with Babyface, Rick Braun, Dave Koz, Norman Brown, and Chuck Loeb. He has a number of film credits *The Prince of Tides, Boyz n the Hood, The Bodyguard, Grand Canyon,* and *Cousins.* He has worked with Luther Vandross, Whitney Houston, George Duke, and his brother, Kevin Whalum.

On June 20, 2014, he was the Jazz Legend honoree of the National Museum of African American Music in Nashville, Tennessee. September 2015, Whalum decided to join the faculty of Visible Music College in Memphis, Tennessee. Kirk has travelled the world; he is fluent in Spanish and French. Kirk is a devout Christian; you can hear and feel the sincerity in his heart when you listen to "Falling in Love with Jesus." Kirk sings and plays on this song. He is accompanied by Jonathan Buttler.

<u>Kirk's Albums</u>

Floppy Disk (1985)- And You Know That (1988)-The Promise (1989)- Mad About the Wolf *from Simply Mad About the Mouse* (1991)-*Cache* (1993)-*In This Life* (1995)-*Joined at the Hip w Bob James* (1996) - *Colors* (1997)-*Gospel According to Jazz: Chapter 1* (1998)-*For You* (1998)-*Unconditional* (2000)-*Hymns in the Garden* (2001)- *The Christmas Message* (2001)- *Grooving w/BWB (Braun, Whalum,* Brown) (2002)-*The Best of Kirk Whalum* (2002)-*Gospel According to Jazz:* Chapter 2 (2002)- *Into My Soul* (2003)- Kirk *Whalum Performs the Babyface Songbook* (2005)-*Ultimate Kirk Whalum* (2007)-*Roundtrip* (2007)-*Promises Made: The Millennium Promise Jazz Project* (2008)- *Everything is Everything: The Music of Donny Hathaway* (2010)-*Romance Language* (2011)-Human *Nature w/BWB* (Braun, Whalum, Brown) (2013)-*The Gospel According to Jazz Chapter IV* (2014)[xciii]

The wisdom of God will take you a long ways in life. Proverbs 29:11 A fool uttereth all his mind, but a wise man keepeth it in till afterwards.

WYNTON MARSALIS

Mr. Marsalis was born October 18, 1961, in New Orleans, Louisiana. He is the son of Ellis Marsalis Jr., a jazz musician. Wynton is a trumpeter, composer, teacher, and music educator. The Lincoln Center in New York City hired him as the artistic director of Jazz. Wynton got an early start in jazz by performing at Fairview Baptist Church. When he was fourteen, he performed with the New Orleans Philharmonic orchestra.

While in high school, he performed with the New Orleans Symphony Brass Quintet, New Orleans Community Concert Band, New Orleans Youth Orchestra, New Orleans Symphony, several jazz bands, and a local funk band, entitled the Creators. He received a grant from the National Endowment of the Arts to spend time with Woody Shaw. Wynton has performed with Sarah Vaughn, Dizzy Gillespie, Sweets Edison, Clark Terry, Sonny Rollins, Ron Carter, Herbie Hancock, Tony Williams, and many others.

Wynton premiered on PBS during an educational television series about jazz in 1996. It was entitled *Marsalis on Music*. National Public Radio aired the first of a 26 week series entitled *Making the Music*. He received the George Foster Peabody Award for the TV show and the radio show. Marsalis has won nine Grammy Awards. He has authored five books *Moving to Higher Ground: How Jazz Can Change your Life*, *Bittersweet Blues of Life*, *To a Young Musician: Letters from the Road*, and *Jazz ABZ (an A to Z collection of poems celebrating jazz greats.)*

Mr. Marsalis won the Pulitzer Prize for Music for his epic oratorio, *Blood on the Fields.*

He won the Netherlands Edison Award. The mayor of Vitoria, Spain awarded him the city's gold medal. A statue is dedicated to Wynton Marsalis in Vitoria-Gasteiz, Spain. In 2009, he received France's highest distinction, the Legion of Honor. In 2011, Marsalis was named cultural correspondence for the news show, *CBS This Morning.*[xciv]

You cannot be lazy while on your journey. Proverbs 26:10 A sluggard says, "There's a lion in the road, a fierce lion roaming the streets!"

KEN FORD

Ken Ford was born November 14, 1968 in St. Louis, Missouri. Mr. Ford grew up in Atlanta, Georgia; he started playing classical violin music at a very early age. He trained on the violin with members of the Atlanta Symphony Orchestra. Before becoming a full time jazz violinist, he worked as an IT programmer during the day.

His musical influences are Stevie Wonder, Noel Pointer, and Jean Luc Ponty. Ford has released four albums- *Burnt Toast* 2001, *Chevelle Lane*, *Right Now 2003*, and the *State of Mind* in 2011.

Ken Ford is avid about keeping music in the school systems. He created the 2010 The Ken Ford Foundation keep arts and music in a child's education. He founded the Dekalb Youth Pops Orchestra.

Mr. Ford has played for President Obama and Michelle Obama, and has played internationally.[xcv]

Proverbs 26:17 Like one who grabs a stray dog by the ears is someone who rushes into a quarrel not their own.

SPECIAL GROUPS/LANDMARK DECISIONS

Thank God for the special groups and landmark decisions, they have left a legacy for blacks and all humanity. The groups are The Underground Railroad, the Tuskegee Airmen, The Little Rock Central High Nine, just to name a few. The groups showed bravery and courage. These individuals were tired at times, but they kept pressing on. In life, nothing comes easy; it requires endurance, persistence, faith, determination, and hope. One thing that made all of these groups successful was unity. We the people in the United States and all over the world must dwell together in unity. Whatever we face in the future we must dwell in unity. God loves all of us. He is a God of righteousness and justice. Be prepared to be brave and to walk in faith. They were brave enough to walk in faith to accomplish their goals. All things work together for the good of them that love the Lord. You know these people had to trust God to overcome the obstacles they encountered.

THE TUSKEGEE AIRMEN

They were the first Black pilots in the U.S. armed forces. The pilots were trained at Tuskegee Institute in Alabama. The Airmen began their training July 19, 1941 on Booker T. Washington's campus.

On March 7, 1942, the first cadets received their wings. They were led by commander, Colonel Benjamin O. Davis Jr. The Colonel Benjamin O. Davis Jr. attended West Point. They flew their first combat mission in North Africa on June 2, 1942 and broke a barrier against Blacks in aerial combat.

The Tuskegee Airmen are known for flying two hundred missions without losing one American heavy bomber to enemy fighter planes. The 450 Black pilots of the 99th, 100th, 301st, and 302nd Fighter Squadrons known collectively as the 332nd Fighter Group were honored on March 24, 1945, by receiving a Presidential Unit Citation for their "outstanding courage, aggressiveness, and combat technique."

There were a total of 992 pilots trained for this project. They had 1578 combat missions, 1267 for the Twelfth Air Force and 311 for the Fifteenth Air Force. The pilot's successes were -112 enemy aircraft destroyed in the air, 150 on the ground, 950 rail cars, trucks/vehicles, 40 boats and barges destroyed.

President Harry Truman enforced Executive Order No. 9981- which declared and enacted equality of treatment and opportunity in the United States Armed Forces, which led to the end of racial segregation in the US military forces. [xcvi]

Lamentations 3:25-The Lord is good to those whose hope is in him, to the one who seeks him.

NEGRO NATIONAL LEAGUE/NEGRO AMERICAN LEAGUE

On February 13 and 14th in the year of 1920 a group of Black baseball club owners met at the Colored YMCA in Kansas City. The owners in attendance Rube Foster- Chicago American Giants, C I Taylor- Indianapolis ABCs, Joe Green- the Chicago Giants, J L Wilkerson -the white owner of the Kansas City Monarchs, Lorenzo S. Cob- St. Louis Giants, and J T Blount- Detroit Stars.

The leagues debut game was May 2, 1920. The Indianapolis ABCs defeated the Chicago Giants 4-2 in front of eight thousand fans at home. The league disbanded in 1931 due to conflicts and the death of Rube Foster on December 9, 1930. The controversy and death did not stop some of these players and coaches. The Negro American League was on the rise.

in 1937 the Negro American League was formed. The NAL league consisted of the Kansas City Monarchs, The St. Louis Stars, The Indianapolis Athletics, The Cincinnati Tigers, The Memphis Red Sox, The Detroit Stars, the Birmingham Black Barons, and the Chicago American Giants. Black baseball teams played each other, they also travelled from town to town within the United States, Cuba, Mexico, and the Dominican Republic to play local Black teams and semi-professional white teams. The Negro National League II started in 1933 and disbanded in 1948. There was an Eastern Colored League formed in 1923 and ended in 1928.

In 1911 Ty Cobb and the Detroit Tigers played a Black baseball team in Cuba. Cobb batted .30 for the five-game series, but John Legend on the Black baseball team averaged .500. Cobb refused to play any more Black teams after the series ended.

NEGRO NATIONAL LEAGUE PENNANTS

1920-1922 Chicago American Giants

1923-1925 Kansas City Monarchs

1926-1927 Chicago American Giants

1928- St. Louis Stars

1929-Kansas City Monarchs

1930-1931-St. Louis Stars

NEGRO AMERICAN LEAGUE PENNANTS

1937-Kansas City Monarchs

1938-Memphis Red Sox

1939-1942 Kansas City Monarchs

1943-1944 Birmingham Black Barons

1945 – Cleveland Buckeyes

1946- Kansas City Monarchs

1947- Cleveland Buckeyes

1948 Birmingham Black Barons[xcvii]

Proverbs 14: 30 A heart at peace gives life to the body, but envy rots the bone.

THE BUFFALO SOLDIERS

The Buffalo Soldiers were formed on September 21, 1866 at Fort Leavenworth, Kansas. They engaged in battle and protected the civilian Indian tribes on the reservations. They were active in building roads, military structures, and took an active part in the Indian Wars in the West.

The Buffalo Soldiers were stationed in outposts in Fort Snelling, Minnesota in the 1880's. The 25th Infantry escorted western migrants, protected mail, stage routes, and fought in attacks on the Apaches, Kiowas, Cheyennes, Comanches, and Arapahos. The 10th Cavalry played an even dramatic role: it was credited with capturing the feared Indian leader Geronimo in 1885. The Buffalo Soldiers had few desertions from their squad and they were devoted to serving. They received fourteen Congressional Medals of Honor for their efforts.

The oldest Buffalo Soldier, Mark Matthews, died on September 6, 2005. He is buried at Arlington National Cemetery. He died at the age of 111 years old.[xcviii]

Proverbs 3: 7- Do not be wise in your own eyes, fear the Lord and shun evil.

CIVIL RIGHTS ACTS OF 1960

The Civil Rights Acts of 1960 strengthened compliance with the Brown versus Board of Education Supreme Court decisions of 1954 to desegregate the South. This law addressed the growing problem of Blacks being denied the right to vote. The act provided the preservation of federal election records, it extends the powers of civil rights, and it appoints voting referees to observe elections, determine if voters were being denied the right to vote. It declares persons qualified to vote have that right on state and local levels.[xcix]

Proverbs 2:11 Discretion will protect you, and understanding will guard you.

VOTING RIGHTS ACT OF 1965

Before the Voting Rights Act of 1965 law was passed, Blacks were denied the right to vote through intimidation, violence, and covert/overt restrictions. The famous Selma to Montgomery March in 1965 demonstrated this. The Alabama state troopers mercilessly beat marchers on their way to the state capital to demand their right to vote.

Congress passed the Voting Rights Act of 1965 signed by President Lyndon Johnson on August 6. It declared unconstitutional any state law that imposed qualifications preventing citizens from voting in federal elections because of their race or color. The act outlawed all tests and taxes required to vote. It created a mechanism for dealing with patterns of race discrimination in voting.

Complaints reached the U.S. attorney general if residents of a certain state were denied the right to vote because of their race or color, or if the ratio of non-white persons to white persons registered to vote suggested that some voters were unregistered because of their race or color. Then the Civil Service Commission is instructed by the attorney general to appoint examiners to maintain lists of persons eligible to vote. The act prevented states from changing their qualifications or their voting districts for a period of five years without review by the attorney general.[c]

Proverbs 24: 26- An honest answer is like a kiss on the lips.

LITTLE ROCK NINE

A group of young black students from Little Rock, Arkansas attended Little Rock Central High. It was a segregated high school in 1957. In 1957, the NAACP registered and selected nine black students based on excellent grades and attendance. The US Supreme Court issued its historic Brown V. Board of Education decision, on May 17, 1954 stating segregated schools were unconstitutional and it called for immediate desegregation of all schools throughout the nation. The NAACP was prepared to act on this decision.

The Little Rock Central Nine students were Minnijean Brown, Elizabeth Eckford, Ernest Green, Thelma Mothershed Wair, Melba Pattillo Beals, Carlotta Walls LaNier, Terrence Roberts, Jefferson Thomas, and Gloria Cecilia Ray. All the students attended Central that year. Ernest Green was the only senior. He graduated that year as the first Black American to graduate from Central High School on May 25, 1958. Dr. Martin Luther King attended the graduation.

Ernest Green was appointed as the assistant Secretary of Housing and Urban Affairs during President Jimmy Carter's administration from 1977 to 1981. Green has been employed as the Managing Director at Lehman Brothers in Washington D. C. He served on the NAACP board and the Winthrop Rockefeller Foundation.

Thelma Mothershed Wair- Graduated from Southern Illinois University in 1964. She received a BA in home economics and received her MS in Guidance and Counseling Education in 1970. Ms. Mothershed taught home economics in the East St. Louis school system. Mrs. Wair taught for twenty-eight years before she left the workforce in 1994.

Melba Pattillo Beals has written a book based on her experiences at Central High School. She published her book in 1995. It's a tell-all book of all the nine students' experience.

Elizabeth Ann Eckord served in the US Army for five years. Ms. Ecford wrote for newspapers in Alabama and Indiana. Currently she works as a probation officer in Little Rock. She was awarded the prestigious Spingarn Medal by the NAACP and The Father Joseph Biltz Award was given to her in 1997.

Carlotta Walls LaNier is the president of the Little Rock Nine Foundation. The foundation has a scholarship dedicated to ensuring equal education for African-Americans. Mrs. Lanier founded LaNier and Company, a real estate brokerage company. She has experience in constructing/remodeling properties and marketing/selling them. Carlotta authored a book *A Mighty Long Way*, with the forward by Bill Clinton.

Terrence Roberts received a doctorate in Psychology. He serves as CEO of Terrence J. Roberts and Associates Management Consulting Firm and maintains a private practice.

Minnijean Brown Trickery was appointed by President Clinton to serve as Deputy Assistant Secretary of the Department of the Interior responsible for diversity. Brown lived in Canada for a number of years; a documentary film was produced in her honor by North-East Pictures in Ottawa-*Journey to Little Rock: The Untold Story of Minnejean Brown Trickery (2002)*.

In 1964, Jefferson Thomas narrated the documentary *Nine from Little Rock* which won an Academy Award. Mr. Thomas worked for Mobil Oil Corporation and later became an accountant for the United States Department of Defense.

Gloria Cecilia Ray received her degree from Illinois Institute of Technology with a bachelor's degree in Chemistry and Mathematics. Mrs. Karlmark worked as documentation expert at a Dutch company and editor of a computer magazine in Europe. Ms. Ray has resided in Sweden and the Netherlands.[ci]

Galatians 5:1 It was for freedom that Christ set us free; therefore keep standing firm and do not be subject again to a yoke of slavery

UNDERGROUND RAILROAD

The Underground Railroad was formed in the early 19th century and reached its peak and height between 1850 and 1860. The estimate is that one hundred thousand slaves escaped via the Underground Railroad. The slaves escaped to free states and Canada. Of course, it was not a real railroad; it was made of meeting places, secret routes, safe houses, transportation, and personal assistance by abolitionist sympathizers. The Abolitionist Movement had people involved in helping slaves to freedom. Be mindful these actions violated state laws and the United States Constitution.

Harriet Tubman is known as the main conductor of the Underground Railroad. She led hundreds of slaves to freedom. Ms. Tubman was a leading abolitionist. She was born in the year of 1820 in Dorchester County, Maryland. She died March 10, 1913. Harriet made sure her family was freed from slavery. The first group of people she freed was her niece Kessiah and her two young children. People called her Moses. There were about 3,200 conductors. The conductors on the railroad came from various backgrounds and included free-born blacks, white abolitionists, former slaves, and Native Americans.

The church community played a major role- the Society of Friends (Quakers), Congregationalists, Wesleyans, Reformed Presbyterians, branches of the Methodist, and American Baptists. Notable people involved in the underground railroad- Anderson Ruffin Abbott, Henry Box Brown, Owen Brown, John

Brown, Samuel Burris, Obadiah Bush, Levi Coffin, Asa Drury, Frederick Douglass, Calvin Fairbank, Matilda Joslyn Gage, Thomas Garrett, William Lloyd Garrison, James Newton Gloucester, Samuel Green, Josiah Bushnell Grinnell, Josiah Henson, James Butler "Wild Bill" Hickok, Laura Smith Haviland, Isaac Hopper, David Hudson, Roger Hooker Leavitt, Jermain Wesley Loguen, Samuel Joseph May, James Mott, Lucretia Coffin Mott, Lucy Higgs Nichols, John Parker, John Wesley Posey, Amy and Isaac Post, John Rankin, Alexander Milton Ross, David Ruggles, Gerritt Smith, William Still, Charles Turner Torrey, Sojourner Truth, Harriett Tubman, Jonathan Walker, Charles Augusta Wheaton, John Greenleaf Whittier, and Martha Coffin Wright.

Notable locations –There were locations Ohio, New York, Massachusetts, Tennessee, Wisconsin, Ontario, Illinois, Iowa, Pennsylvania, Michigan, Connecticut, Nova Scotia, Nebraska, Indiana, Toronto, Kansas Westfield, Indiana, West Nyack, New York, Wheaton College, Wheaton, Illinois, Wilmington, Delaware, and Windsor, Ontario.[cii]

Galatians 6:9 And let us not be weary in well doing, for in due season we shall reap, if we faint not.

MINISTRIES/PREACHERS

Ephesians 4:11, 12 AMP version- And (his gifts to the church were varied and) He Himself self-appointed some as apostles (special messengers, representatives), some as prophets (who speak a new message from God to the people), some as evangelists (who spread the good news of salvation), and some as pastors and teachers (to shepherd and guide and instruct). (and He did this) to fully equip and perfect the saints (God's people) for works of service, to build up of the body of Christ (the church).

2 Corinthians 3:6 AMP He has qualified us (making us sufficient) as ministers of a new covenant (of salvation through Christ), not of the letter (of a written code) but of the Spirit; for the letter (of the Law) kills *by revealing sin and demanding obedience), but the 'spirit gives life.

If you know God has called you to be spokespersons for him, do not run. God is gentle but he will continue to knock at your heart. Do it afraid. I pray you do not run from the call, people have made the decision to be ministers, preachers, pastors, and bishops. They walked in faith, even though they walked in faith does not mean they were not afraid.

BISHOP DALE C. BRONNER

Bishop Dale Carnegie Bronner is the presiding bishop of Word of Faith Family Cathedral in Austell, Georgia. He is the son of the late Nathaniel Hawthorne Bronner Sr. and Mrs. Robbie Bronner and the fourth of six sons.

He resides in metro Atlanta area and married to Dr. Nina Bronner. They are the proud parents of four daughters and one son.

Bishop Bronner is a graduate of Morehouse College and earned his doctor of Ministry degree from Christian Life School of Theology.

Dale Carnegie Bronner serves on the board of directors of Bronner Brothers Manufacturing Company. This company has been in the hair care business for over sixty years. It is a multi-million dollar family-owned corporation.

Mr. Bronner is an accomplished author of several books. He has travelled the world to speak God's word. His books are entitled *Get a Grip*, *Guard your Gates*, *A Check up From the Neck Up*, *Treasure your Silent Years*, *Home Remedies*, *Pass the Baton*, and *Change your Trajectory*.

The worship services for Word of Faith appear on Daystar Television, AIB Network, TBN Broadcasting, and local channels in Atlanta. Bishop Bronner has ministered all over the world. His mission is to reach the lost and teach the found.

<u>Quotes by Bishop Bronner:</u>

Sometimes, the problem comes from you, which means that you also have the power to change it.

Prayer will: Get you in, Get you out, Get you thru, never underestimate the power of prayer.

Never let a broken wing stop you from planning your next flight! You will heal and fly again!

If you lack conviction on the inside you will lack commitment on the outside.

Faith is not a tool to change the will of God but to usher it into manifestation!

Discipline is doing what you know needs to be done even if you don't want to do it.

Sometimes when God really wants to promote your life he'll schedule an enemy.[ciii]

Philippians 2:21 For me to live is Christ and to die is gain.

TD JAKES

Bishop TD Jakes is a well-known minister located in metro Dallas in the state of Texas. He is the Bishop and founder of Potter's House Christian Fellowship. Bishop Jakes is a pastor, teacher, author, producer, etc. He was born as Thomas Dexter Jakes in South Charleston, West Virginia on June 9, 1957. His wife's name is Serita Jakes and his parents are Ernest Jakes Sr. and Odith Jakes.

Jakes served as the pastor of Greater Emanuel Temple of Faith in 1980. It was in Smithers, West Virginia; the church only had ten members.

In 1982, he became the pastor of the Greater Emanuel Temple of Faith. It was a small Montgomery, West Virginia independent Pentecostal church.

Currently, he presides over the Potter's House. It has more than thirty thousand members and over fifty outreach ministries.

TD Jakes has produced these movies- *Woman thou Art Loosed*, *Jumping the Broom*, *Heaven is for Real*, *Not Easily Broken*, and *Sparkle*. Bishop Jakes has an inspirational wisdom fulfilled talk show on the Oprah Winfrey Network.

He and his church family hold conferences for men and women all over the United States of America. T. D. Jakes has an interest in justice and righteousness in the United States of America. The Dallas community respects him and calls on him to pray. Bishop

Jakes can be heard on Daystar Network, TBN Network, and The Word Network.

Famous Quotes

I think the first step is to understand that forgiveness does not exonerate the perpetrator. Forgiveness liberates the victim. It's a gift you give yourself.

It is your passion that empowers you to be able to do that thing you were created to do.

I don't think that you can let the storms of life overwhelm you. When you do that, you are no better than the craziness that caused you to be under attack.[civ]

Ephesians 6: 10 Finally, my brethren, be strong in the Lord, and in the power of his might.

FREDERICK K. C. PRICE

Frederick K. C. Price has been the apostle of Crenshaw Christian Center located In California since 1970. He was born January 3, 1932. His church is called the dome that faith built. Mr. Price married Betty Price in 1953. They met while attending Dorsey High School. They have four children. His son Frederick Kenneth Price serves as a senior pastor.

The churches Ever Increasing Faith broadcast has aired in millions of homes throughout the United States.

Mr. Price founded the Fellowship of International Christian Word of Faith Ministries (FICWFM). It consists of churches and ministers from all over the United States and a few countries. They meet in different regions throughout the year and hold an annual convention.

Frederick K. C. Price is the author of many books, there are plenty not listed:

Race, Religion, and Racism Vol 1 and Vol 2., *Faith's Greatest Enemies*, *How Faith Works*, *The Holy Spirit: The Helper We all Need*, *Answered Prayer Guaranteed!*: The Power of Praying with Faith *Prosperity: Good News for God's People*, *How to Obtain Strong Faith: Six Principles*, *The Christian Family: Practical Insight for Family Living*, *Faith, Foolishness, or Presumption?*[cv]

Philippians 2: 14 Do all things without grumbling or disputing.

CREFLO DOLLAR JR.

Pastor Dollar was born Creflo Augustus Dollar Jr. on January 28, 1962. His father was Creflo Dollar Sr. Creflo was reared in the Baptist church and is married to Taffi Dollar. They have five children Jordan, Lauren, Gregory, Alexandria, and Jeremy.

Pastor Dollar received a Bachelor of Science degree in education from West Georgia College in Carrolton, Georgia. He founded World Changers Church in 1986. Worlds Changers International has weekly Bible study meetings and meets every Sunday. World Changers host conferences all over the United States and internationally.

The services can be seen on TV and heard on the radio. Pastor Creflo speaks directly from the word of God and is a bold man of God and full of faith. He believes in ministry to the mind, soul, and spirit.

Creflo Dollar has a magazine publication entitled *Change*, and he is the author of many books: Before *the Ring Resource Guide, Effective Faith 10 steps That will Revolutionize Your Walk with God, Building your Life through Faith, Understanding Names of God, Live without Fear* and many more.

Creflo Dollar Ministries has offices in Canada, Europe, Asia Pacific, USA, and South Africa.[cvi]

I Thessalonians 5: Rejoice always.

SINGERS

There are singers and there are singers. Some singers can pick out parts to a song very quickly. It is nothing but the gift of God. If you have the gift of singing, I pray that you will allow God to use you in a mighty way. God has given you a unique gift, walk in it. Everyone has their own unique sound. It's not necessary to attempt to copy anyone's sound. You have been blessed with a unique gift. The word of God says your gift will make room for you. I pray that you will protect and preserve your voice and vocal chords at all times.

People have sung for ages. God talks about singing in the Bible.

Psalms 68:32 -Sing to God, you kingdom of the earth, sing praise to the Lord.

Zechariah 2:10- Sing and rejoice, O daughter of Zion: for, lo, I come, and I will dwell in the midst of thee, saith the Lord.

Ephesians 5:19- Speaking to yourselves in psalms and hymns and spiritual songs, singing and making melody in your heart to the Lord.

MARIAN ANDERSON

Marian Anderson was born February 27, 1897 in Philadelphia, Pennsylvania. Both her parents were devout Christians, and her family was active in the Union Baptist Church in South Philadelphia.

Marian had the People's Chorus, the pastor of her church Reverend Wesley Parks, along with other leaders of the black community raise money so she could take singing lessons with Mary Saunders Patterson. Ms. Anderson attended South Philadelphia High School. Her father was accidentally struck on the head while at work and killed right before Christmas in 1909.

Marian was an American contralto, and a celebrated singer. She sang throughout the United States and Europe including singing with famous orchestras and recited in major music venues.

The great Italian conductor Arturo Toscanini told her, "Yours is a voice such as one hears once in a hundred years." Alan Blyth said, "Her voice was a rich, vibrant contralto of intrinsic beauty."

Marian was an important figure for black artists to overcome racial prejudice in the United States. In 1939, The Daughters of the American Revolution (DAR) refused permission for Anderson to sing to an integrated audience in the Constitution Hall.

President Roosevelt and the first lady were instrumental in getting Marian a performance at the Lincoln Memorial on April 9, 1939. There was a crowd of more than 75,000 people and a radio audience in the millions.

Anderson worked for several years as a delegate to the United Nations Human Rights Committee and as a goodwill ambassador for the United States. In the 1960's, she participated in the civil rights movement and she sang at the March on Washington for Jobs and Freedom in 1963.

Awards and Honors

Presidential Medal of Freedom in 1963

Kennedy Center in 1978

National Medal of Arts in 1986

Grammy Lifetime Achievement Award in 1991

Marian experienced freedom and fame in Europe. She was not faced with racial prejudices as she received in America. Albert Einstein hosted Marian Anderson when she was denied hotel accommodations in the United States. Marian Anderson died April 8, 1993.[cvii]

I Timothy 6:17 NASB Instruct those who are rich in this present world not to be conceited or to fix their hope on the uncertainty of riches but on God, who richly supplies us with all things to enjoy.

ANDRAE CROUCH

Andrae Edward Crouch was born July 1, 1942 in San Francisco, California. He has a twin sister Sandra Crouch. Their parents are Benjamin and Catherine Crouch. His parents were entrepreneurs, they owned a dry cleaners and a restaurant business. Crouch's parents had a street ministry, a hospital, and prison ministry. At the age of eleven, Crouch played the piano by ear during a service his father was ministering at.

In 1960 Crouch founded a group, Church of God in Christ Singers. The group included Billy Preston. With this group he recorded "The Blood Will Never Lost its Power." Crouch was in two more groups, The Disciples and the Imperials.

In 1979, Crouch began his solo career. Throughout Crouch's career he was a singer, songwriter, arranger, record producer, choir director, and pastor. He played the piano and the organ.

His musical arrangements were heard in the films *The Lion King*, *The Color Purple*, and the TV series *Amen*. He was inducted into the Gospel Music Hall of Fame in 1998 and in the same year he received a star on the Hollywood Walk of Fame. He won seven Grammies and four GMA Dove Awards. Crouch received the ASCAP, Billboard, and NAACP Awards.

Recordings:

Andrae Crouch and The Disciples: 1969 *Take the Message Everywhere* (Light records), 1971 *Keep on Singin,* 1972 *Soulfully,* 1973: *Live at Carnegie Hall,* 1975 *Take me Back,* 1976 *This is another Day,* and 1978 *Live in London.* Solo recordings 1973 *Just Andrae,*1979 *I'll be thinking of you,* 1981 *Don't give up,* 1982 *Finally,* 1984 *No Time to Lose,* 1986 *Autograph,* 1994 *Mercy,* 1997 *Pray,* 1998 *Gift of Christmas,* 2006 *Mighty Wind,* 2011 *The Journey,* 2013 *Live In Los Angeles*[cviii]

I Thessalonians 5: 17 Pray without ceasing.

WALTER HAWKINS

Walter Hawkins is a legend in the gospel industry. Walter was born May 18, 1949 in Oakland, California. He was a singer, songwriter, producer, a pastor, and became a bishop in 1992. Mr. Hawkins played the piano and the keyboard. He had five brothers and sisters. He married Tramaine Hawkins. They had two children, Walter "Jamie" Hawkins Jr. and a daughter Trystan Hawkins.

Walter had a brother named Edwin Hawkins. Edwin and Walter formed and founded the Edwin Hawkins Singers. This effort produced the song "Oh Happy Day," this song crossed over into the mainstream music charts. After this endeavor, Walker Hawkins established the Love Center Church in Oakland, California. His church choir recorded the Love Alive series, which sold over a million copies from the 1970s through the 1990s. *The Love Alive IV* released in 1990 and it stayed on the Billboard Gospel Album charts. It stayed on the chart for thirty-three weeks. Walter Hawkins produced or collaborated on over one hundred sixteen hit songs. They were listed on the Billboard Gospel Music charts. Walter has songs and albums that date from 1972 through 2010.

Walter received numerous awards and was nominated for nine Grammy Awards. He won the 1981 Grammy for Best Gospel Performance, Contemporary or Inspirational for the special project *The Lord's Prayer*.

Hawkins won three Gospel Music Association Dove Awards:

1980: Soul Gospel Album of the year for *Love Alive II*. Walter Hawkins and the Love Center Choir.

1982 Contemporary Gospel Album of the Year for *The Hawkins Family Live*.

1991 Traditional Song of the Year for *The Potter's House* (co songwriter).

He won two Stellar Awards- 1)2006 Traditional Male Vocalist of the Year.

2) 2006 Traditional CD of the Year for a *Song in My Heart*.

Bishop Walter Hawkins died on July 11, 2010.[cix]

I Thessalonians 5: 18 In everything give thanks, for this is the God's will for you in Christ Jesus.

THOMAS DORSEY

Thomas Andrew Dorsey was born July 1, 1899 and died January 23, 1993. He was known as the father of black gospel music. Songs written with his style of music was known as the Dorsey's. Dorsey was born in Villa Rica, Georgia. His father was a minister and his mother was a piano teacher.

Initially, he played blues on the piano, but later played gospel and the blues. Dorsey lived in Chicago, Illinois. He served as the musical director of Pilgrim Baptist Church in Chicago, Illinois and was the musical director until 1970.

Mr. Dorsey is known for *Take my Hand, Precious Lord*, and *Peace in the Valley*. Mahalia Jackson was the solo artist for *Take My Hand, Precious Lord*.

Dorsey opened the first black gospel music publishing company, Dorsey House of Music. He started it because he was not satisfied with the established publishers. Dorsey started his own choir and was the founder and first president of the National Convention of Gospel Choirs and Choruses.

He was the first African American elected to the Nashville Songwriters Hall of Fame, and the first in the Gospel Music Association's Living Hall of Fame. Dorsey's papers are preserved at Fisk University.

Thomas died in Chicago, Illinois.[cx]

II Thessalonians 2:3 The grace of our Lord Jesus Christ be with you all.

MAHALIA JACKSON

Mahalia Jackson was thought of internationally as a gospel singer and a civil rights activist. She was determined to sing for God only, which gave her notoriety. Mahalia said, "I sing God's music because it makes me feel free". "It gives me hope. With the blues, when you finish, you still have the blues."

Ms. Jackson was born October 26, 1911, and she died January 27, 1972. Mahalia recorded over thirty albums for Columbia Records. In 1927, at the age of sixteen, Jackson moved to Chicago, Illinois. In the year of 1929, she met the great composer Thomas A. Dorsey. He advised her musically. They began touring together, and Dorsey's song "Take My Hand Precious Lord" became her signature song.

Mahalia had several recordings which include *You Better Run Run Run, Move on Up a Little Higher, Silent Night, Amazing Grace, I can Put my Trust in Jesus, Walk with Me, Go Tell it On the Mountain, The Lord's Prayer, How I Got Over, His Eye is On the Sparrow*, and *I Believe*.

Mahalia sung in Montgomery, Alabama, at a rally to raise money for the Montgomery bus boycott. She sang "I've Heard of a City Called Heaven, Move on Up a Little Higher, and Silent Night." There was a great timeout, and they were happy with the amount of money raised.

Jackson was the first African American to sing at Carnegie Hall.

At the March on Washington for Jobs and Freedom in 1963 Jackson performed "I been Buked and I Been Scorned," before King gave his *I Have a Dream Speech*. Jackson's last song was "What the World Needs Now", in 1969 and the next year she and Louis Armstrong performed together "Just A Closer Walk with Thee." She appeared on the *Flip Wilson Show*, and on *Sesame Street*.

Jackson died in Chicago on January 27, 1972.[cxi]

I Timothy 4:14 Do not neglect the spiritual gift within you, which was bestowed on you through prophetic utterance with the laying on of hands by the presbytery.

SHIRLEY ANN CAESAR WILLIAMS

Ms. Caesar is known professionally as Shirley Caesar. She was born October 13, 1938 in Durham, North Carolina. Shirley started singing at a very young age, she sang with the caravans along with Albertina Walker, Dorothy Norwood, and James Cleveland.

Caesar has recorded over forty albums and has been recording since the age of twelve. Pastor Caesar is a graduate of Shaw University, where she earned a Bachelor's of Science degree in Business Administration. As of 2016, she has sung for every president of the United States since Jimmy Carter.

Pastor Caesar has been the pastor of Mt. Calvary Word of Faith Church in Raleigh, North Carolina for more than twenty years.

Shirley has recorded many songs, such as "I Remember Mama, Jesus I Love Calling your Name, Hold my Mule, Playground in Heaven Music Video, I Feel Like Praising Him, Nobody, Favor, The Praying Slave Lady, How Many will be Remembered, Satan We're Gonna Tear your Kingdom Down, Been so Good, Amazing Grace, Teach Me Master, Heaven, and many more."

 She has recorded commercials for MCI Communications and has been in musicals- *Mama I want to Sing, Sing: Mama 2 and Born to Sing: Mama 3.*

Shirley Caesar has won eleven Grammy Awards, fourteen Stellar Awards, eighteen Dove Awards, one RIAA Award, an Essence Award, NAACP

Achievement Award, and many more.[cxii]

I Timothy 6:10 For the love of money is a root of all sorts of evil, and some by longing for it have wandered away from the faith and pierced themselves with many griefs.

PAUL ROBESON

Paul Robeson was born in Princeton, New Jersey in the year of 1898 to Reverend William Drew Robeson and Maria Louisa Bustill. His mother was mixed; she was related to a prominent Quaker family. Her ancestry was mixed of African, Anglo-American, and Lenape. Robeson's father escaped from slavery as a teen and became the minister of Princeton's Witherspoon Street Presbyterian Church in 1881. Robeson had three brothers and one sister.

During his high school years, Robeson performed in *Julius Caesar*, *Othello*, and sang in the chorus. He excelled in football, basketball, baseball, and track. Before he graduated from high school, he won a state-wide academic contest for a scholarship to Rutgers.

Robeson finished Rutgers with four annual oratorical triumphs, varsity letters in multiple sports, and he was class valedictorian.

After a year of dating Eslanda "Essie" Goode he married her in August 1921. They had one son together. Paul was recruited to play NFL football while he studied law. He toured off Broadway in a production entitled *Shuffle Along* and then he joined *Taboo* in Britain. Robeson worked briefly as a lawyer, but quit due to extant racism.

Robeson became the first black actor cast as *Othello* in Britain.

You can classify him as a singer, actor, social activist, lawyer, and athlete.[cxiii]

I Timothy 6: 12 Fight the good fight of faith, lay hold on eternal life, whereunto thou art also called, and has professed a good profession before many witnesses.

YOLANDA ADAMS

Yolanda Yvette Adams was born August 27, 1961 in Houston, Texas. Her father died when she was in her early teens. She attended Sterling High School in Houston, Texas.

In her early years she sung with the Southeast Inspirational Choir. Her signature song with the group was "My Liberty." Yolanda Adams was influenced by Thomas Whitfield and the Sound of Gospel which led her to singing with the Southeast Inspirational Choir. Yolanda was spotlighted with Edwin Hawkins Music and Arts Seminar Choir, which released *Give Us Peace*.

Yolanda eventually signed a contract with Sound of Gospel which yielded her first album *Just As I Am* in 1987. Ben Tankard discovered her in 1990, she signed to his independent label Tribute Records and she produced her *Through the Storm* project.

"The Battle is the Lord's", is known as her signature song. Yolanda has won four Grammy Awards, sixteen Stellar Gospel Awards, four Dove Awards, one American Music Award, seven NAACP Image Awards, One Soul Train Music Award, and five BET Awards.

Adams released her first book *Points of Power in 2010.*

She has one daughter Taylor Ayanna Crawford.

Yolanda Adams produced *Yolanda Adams Morning Show* for more than three years; it was a nationally syndicated radio show.

Yolanda Adams sung "Spirit in the Dark" to President Barack Obama and First Lady Michelle Obama at the Smithsonian Salute to Ray Charles" at the White House.

•Albums by Yolanda:

- 1987: *Just as I Am*
- 1991: *Through the Storm*
- 1993: *Save the World*
- 1995: *More Than A Melody*
- 1997: *Yolanda Live in Washington*
- 1998: *Songs from the Heart*
- 1999: *Mountain High …Valley Low*
- 2000: *Christmas with Yolanda Adams*
- 2001: *The Experience*
- 2001: *Believe*
- 2005: *Day by Day*
- 2007: *What a Wonderful Time*
- 2011: *Becoming*
- 2015 *How Awesome is Our God with Israel New Breed*

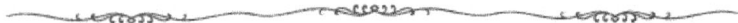

Hebrews 2:13 And again, I will put my trust in Him.

ARETHA FRANKLIN

Aretha Franklin was born March 25, 1942 in Memphis, Tennessee. Aretha is worth sixty million dollars. Her parents are Barbara Siggers Franklin and C.L. Franklin. Franklin's father was a Baptist preacher. Ms. Franklin was married to Glynn Turman from 1978 to 1984 and Ted White from 1961 to 1969. She has four children Ted White Jr., Clarence Franklin, Edward Franklin, and Kecalf Cunningham.

Aretha is a gifted, talented singer and pianist. Aretha toured with her father's traveling revival show. After that Aretha signed with Columbia Records in New York. In 1987 she became the first female artist to be inducted into the Rock and Roll Hall of Fame. In 2008, Franklin won her 18th Grammy Award.

"I Never Loved a Man (The Way I Love You)," reached number one on R& B and pop charts and she won her first two Grammy Awards. Other top ten hits include "Baby I love you, Think, Chain of Fools, I Say a Little Prayer, Respect, and You Make Me Feel Like a Natural Woman."

Aretha has appeared in two movies *The Blues Brothers* in 1980 and *Blue Brothers* 2000. In 1982's *Jump to It* an album enjoyed huge success on the R & B charts. This song earned her a Grammy nomination. In 1985, Franklin released "Who's Zoomin

Who?" In 1986 her duet with George Michael went gold, "I Knew You Were Waiting (For Me)."

257

In 1993 she sang at the inauguration of Bill Clinton and in 1994, she was honored with a Grammy Lifetime Achievement Award. Ms. Franklin is known as the Queen of Soul.

Aretha Franklin quote:

> *Being a singer is a natural gift. It means I'm using it to the highest degree possible the gift that God gave me to use. I'm happy with that.*

Philippians 4:13 I can do all things through Christ which strengtheneth me.

LAWYERS/ATTORNEYS

God will lead and guide you through preparing for becoming a lawyer/attorney. If you listen to him, he will help you make wise decisions. The United States need people that study the law. Justice needs to be served; attorneys and lawyers assist in getting this accomplished. Both lawyers and attorneys have studied the law, the only difference is attorneys have passed the bar exams. Lawyers can give legal advice but cannot provide legal representation. I encourage you to go all the way, pass the bar exam. It is never too late to go to school; you can be twenty, thirty, forty, fifty, sixty, or seventy. It is never too late in God's eyes.

God is a God of justice. He talks about justice in the Bible.

Ruth 4:7 – (Now in earlier times in Israel, for the redemption and transfer of property to become final, one party took off his sandal and gave it to the other. This was the method of legalizing transactions in Israel.)

Exodus 23:6- Do not deny justice to your poor people in their lawsuits.

Proverbs 21:15- When justice is done, it brings joy to the righteous but terror to evildoers.

Exodus 23:2- Do not follow the crowd in doing wrong. When you give testimony in a lawsuit, do not pervert justice by siding with the crowd.

God bless you in your endeavors. Trust God, he will lead and guide you.

THURGOOD MARSHALL

Thurgood Marshall was born July 2, 1908 in Baltimore, Maryland. He was an Associate Justice of the Supreme Court of the United States. His parents are Norma Africa Marshall and William Marshall. He had two sons Thurgood Marshall Jr. and John.

Thurgood was a Civil Rights Activist and the first Black American Supreme Court Justice. Thurgood studied law at Howard University; he graduated first in his class.

Marshall's victories:

Murray v. Pearson- It was against the University of Maryland. The school he could not attend. He challenged their segregation policy. He opened the door to equal education for generations of Maryland students.

The National Association for the Advancement of Colored People. He became chief counsel for the NAACP. The notorious Brown V. Board of Education, yielded a unanimous decision in favor of integrating schools.

1961 -President John F. Kennedy appointed him to the 2nd Circuit Court of Appeals in 1961.

1961- Defends civil rights demonstrators, winning Supreme Circuit Court victory in Garner V. Louisiana.

1965- He became the first black U.S. solicitor general. He won 14 of the 19 cases he argued for the nation.

1966- President Lyndon B. Johnson to the US Supreme Court said this about Thurgood. "The right thing to do, the right time to do it, the right man and the right place."

Marshall retired in 1991, and on January 24, 1993 he died. A few months after his death, President Bill Clinton awarded Marshall the Presidential Medal of Freedom, the nation's highest civilian honor.[cxiv]

Romans 8:28 And we know that all things work together for good to them who are the called according to his purpose.

ANTHONY KAPEL VAN JONES

Anthony Kapel Van Jones is an American political activist commentator, author, and attorney. Mr. Jones was born September 20, 1968 in Jackson, Tennessee. He is married to Jana Carter. He co-founded Dream Corps, a non-profit organization which focuses on social justice. He owns and operates three advocacy projects #cut50, #YesWeCode and Green for All.

Mr. Jones has authored two New York Best-selling books, *The Green Collar Economy* and *Rebuild the Dream.* Van Jones worked with President Obama as his special advisor on Green Jobs, as an Associate Professor at Princeton University, and a co-host of CNN's political debate show *Crossfire. Time* magazine named Jones as one of the most influential people in the world and he received the NAACP President's award in 2010.

Jones attended the University of Tennessee at Martin and Yale Law School. Jones moved to San Francisco after he graduated from law school. He became a member of a socialist collective called Standing Together to Organize a Revolutionary Movement (STORM) that protested against police brutality.

HONORS

In 2012 *Rolling Stone* Magazine 12 Leaders who get things done, 2013 *The Root* Magazine 100 Honorees and 2013 *Ebony* Magazine's Power   100.

<u>Quote by Jones:</u>

I cannot in good conscience ask my colleagues to expend precious time and energy defending or explaining my past. We need all hands on deck, fighting for the future.[cxv]

Hebrews 3:4 For every house is built by someone, but the builder of all things is God.

LORETTA ELIZABETH LYNCH

Loretta Lynch was born May 21, 1959 in Greensboro, North Carolina. Her mother was a school librarian, and her father a minister. One of Loretta's favorite things to do was watch court proceeding in the courthouse of Durham, North Carolina. Her parents told her stories of her grandfather, a pastor and sharecropper who helped people move to the north to escape prosecutions under the Jim Crow laws.

Ms. Lynch graduated from Harvard College in 1981 with a Bachelor's of Arts in English and American literature and received a Juris Doctor from Harvard Law School in 1984.

Her first job was a litigator for Cahill Gordon & Reindel. She became a violent-crime prosecutor in the US Attorney's office in 1990. President Bill Clinton nominated her to serve as the US Attorney for the Eastern District of New York. Loretta oversaw prosecution of New York City police officers in the Abner Louima case.

On November 8, 2014, President Barack Obama nominated her for the position of U.S. Attorney General to succeed Eric Holder. Her nomination process was the longest in history. It took 166 days to be confirmed for the position. Ms. Lynch is the 83rd United States Attorney General. The confirmation for the position took place on April 3, 2015.[cxvi]

Hebrews 11:30 By faith the walls of Jericho fell down after they had been encircled for seven days.

ERIC HOLDER

Eric Himpton Holder Jr. was born January 21, 1951 in Bronx, New York. He attended Stuyvesant High School, Columbia University, and Columbia Law School Columbia College of Columbia University in the City of New York.

Mr. Holder married Sharon Malone in 1990. They have three children Brooke Holder, Maya Holder, and Eric Holder.

In the year of 1997, Eric was nominated to be the Deputy Attorney General under Janet Reno during the Clinton Administration. In the year of 2001 and until he became Attorney General Mr. Holder worked as an attorney at Covington & Burling in Washington, D. C. He represented clients such as Merck and the National Football League.

Mr. Holder served as the 82nd Attorney General of the United States of America. He served under the presidency of Barack Obama. He served as the attorney general from 2009 to 2015. Before becoming attorney general he served as a judge of the Superior Court of the District of Columbia and as US Attorney for the District of Columbia.

In addition, he was senior legal advisor to Barack Obama during his presidential campaign and one of three members of Obama's vice-presidential selection committee.

Holder has spoken honestly and in very frank terms about racism in the United States. He stands for civil rights and voting rights.

Recently Holder has played a major part in black lives matters. Mr. Holder is authoring a book entitled, *Pursing Justice*. [cxvii]

Hebrews 13:5, 6 Never will I leave you, never will I forsake you. So we say with confidence, The Lord is my helper, I will not be afraid, What can mere mortals do to me?

JOHNNY L COCHRAN

Johnny L Cochran was born October 2, 1937 in Shreveport, Louisiana. His parents were entrepreneurs, his father sold insurance and his mother sold Avon products. In 1949, the family relocated to Los Angeles. Cochran was destined for greatness; he graduated first in his class in 1955.

In 1959, he received his Bachelor of Science degree in business administration from UCLA. He also received Juris Doctor at the Loyola Marymount University School of Law In 1962. Johnny was inspired by Thurgood Marshall and the legal victory he won in Brown versus Board of Education. Cochran felt being a lawyer was a calling, a double opportunity to work for what he considered being right and to challenge what he considered wrong, he could make a difference by practicing law.

Johnny authored a book *In A Lawyer's Life*. Cochran passed the bar in 1963. Two years later, he entered private practice and soon opened his own firm, Cochran, Atkins & Evans, in rural Woodstock, Illinois. He was litigating a number of high-profile police brutality and criminal cases.

In 1978, he started a practice, reinventing himself as 'THE BEST IN THE WEST" by opening the Johnnie L. Cochran, Jr. law firm. The Johnnie Cochran Firm still exists today more than ten years after his death. Cochran is known for being an attorney in the OJ Simpson case. Mr. Cochran died March 29, 2005. The Cochran Firm is still operational after his death. What a legacy![cxviii]

But without faith it is impossible to please him, for he that cometh to God must believe that he is, and that he is a rewarder of them that diligently seek him.

PUBLICATIONS

The publications in this section spread the news for the Black culture. There are black publications all over the United States. They have provided information we needed for ages. Some of them are African American News and Issues, Atlanta Daily World, Atlanta Tribune, Baltimore Times, Birmingham Times, Boston-Bay State Banner, Carolina Peacemaker, Chicago Defender, Dallas Examiner, Los Angeles Sentinel, Milwaukee Courier, San Francisco Bay View, plus many more. Our race needed these publications to inform and educate us.

News in the biblical days was spread by word of mouth.

Mark 1:28 News about him spread quickly over the whole region of Galilee.

Proverbs 25:25 Like cold water to a weary soul is good news from a distant land.

Luke 3:18- And with many other words John exhorted the people and proclaimed the good news to them.

Luke 4:43- But he said, "I must proclaim the good news of the kingdom of God to the other towns also, because that is why I was sent."

EBONY

Ebony got its start November 1, 1945. It was created by John H. Johnson. The magazine focused then and now on the needs and lifestyles of black Americans. The content centered on business, health, entertainment, occupation, sports, black history, and personalities.

In the 1950's it ran a column by Dr. Martin Luther King entitled "Advice for Living." By the 1960's the focus was on civil rights. Ebony provided a much needed forum for blacks.

In 1972, the magazine Publishers Association named Johnson as the magazine publisher of the year. Every year the magazine featured the one hundred most influential blacks in America.

Ebony magazine was a necessity for black households. The magazine published the twenty-five Coolest Brothers of All Time. This was done August 2008. The personalities featured were President Obama, Jay-Z, Denzel Washington, Prince, Samuel Jackson, Marvin Gaye, Muhammad Ali, and Billy Dee Williams. The magazine had a sixty-fifth anniversary edition in the year of 2010. It featured Taraji P. Henson, Samuel L. Jackson, Usher and Mary J. Blige. All of these articles were big successes for the magazine.

The magazine is online under Ebony.com.[cxix]

Romans 8:31 NASB What then shall we say to these things? If God is for us who is against us?

JET

Jet magazine was a must have in the 50's 60's 70's and 80's. It was founded in 1951 by John H. Johnson. He worked for the Johnson Publishing Company in Chicago, Illinois. The original name was *The Weekly Negro News Magazine*. In its early years, it covered the Emmett Till murder, the Montgomery Bus Boycott, and Martin Luther King Jr.

The first issue was published November 1, 1951 and the final issue was June 2014. It is presently a digital magazine. Redd Foxx called the magazine "the Negro Bible." The men loved to receive the magazine to look at the weekly bathing suit model.

Jet magazine wrote about fashion/beauty tips, entertainment news, dating advice, political coverage, health tips, and diet guides.

The magazine was small in size and pages. It did not take long to read it, but it was very informative.

It has a presence on the World Wide Web. The magazine's website is http:www.jetmag.com.[cxx]

Romans 10:11 NASB For the scripture says, Whoever believes in Him will not be disappointed."

ESSENCE

Essence is a monthly publication for black women. It is a monthly publication. Edward Lewis, Clarence O. Smith, Cecil Hollingsworth, and Johnathan Blount founded Essence Communications Inc. in 1968. The magazine began publishing in May 1970. The publication reached eight million readers in the United States, The Caribbean, Canada, the United Kingdom, and the English-speaking African nations.

The *Essence* brand branched into book publishing, broadcasting, eyewear, hosiery, and its very own fashion catalogue. A music festival was created to top it all, entitled the Essence Musical Festival. There is always plenty of music and seminars. It's held in New Orleans, Louisiana.

Editors

- Ruth Ross (1975)
- Ida Lewis (1970–71)
- Marcia Ann Gillespie (1971–80)
- Susan L. Taylor (1981–2000)
- Monique Greenwood (2000)
- Diane Weathers (2000–05)
- Angela Burt-Murray (2005–10)
- Constance C. R. White (2011–13)
- Vanessa K. Bush (2013–present)

In 2008, *Essence* won twelve New York Association of Black Journalists awards in the Investigative, General Feature, International, Business/Technology, Science/Health, Arts / Entertainment, Personal Commentary, Public Affairs and Online categories.[cxxi]

Romans 12:18 If it be possible, as much as lieth in you, live peaceably with all men.

ENDNOTES

[i] Mlkonline speeches.com
[ii] www.dictionary.com
[iii] The Bible all versions all scriptures in book
www.biblegateway.com

[iv] www.biograpy.com
[v] www.imdb.com
[vi] www.biograpy.com
[vii] Www.imdbpro.com
[viii] www.imdb.com
[ix] www.tv.com
[x] www.rottentomatoes.com
[xi] www.biography.com
[xii] www.blackpast.org
[xiii] www.imdb.com
[xiv] Poets.org
[xv] www.nytimes.com
[xvi] Poets.org
[xvii] www.britannica.com
[xviii] www.toiderricotte.com
[xix] www.read.gov
[xx] www.poetryoutloud.org

[xxi] www.biography.com
[xxii] www.britannica.com
[xxiii] www.historymakers.com
[xxiv] www.blackinventors.com
[xxv] www.african-american-scientists.com
[xxvi] www.notablebiographies.com

[xxvii] Blackinventor.com
[xxviii] Great Negroes Past and Present by Russell Adams
[xxix] Fenomlife.com
[xxx] www.hypress.net, Wikipedia.org, blackamericaweb.com
[xxxi] Great Negroes Past and Present by Russell Adams
[xxxii] www.biography.com

xxxiii www.blackpast.org

xxxiv www.nasa.gov, www.wikipedia.org

xxxv Blackinventor.com, www.biography.com

xxxvi Great Negroes Past and Present by Russell Adams

xxxvii Great Negroes Past and Present by Russell Adams

xxxviii Great Negroes Past and Present by Russell Adams

xxxix Great Negroes Past and Present by Russell Adams

xl Great Negroes Past and Present by Russell Adams

xli NAACP: History: Roy Wilkins

xlii www.biography.com

xliii www.britannica.com

xliv www.biography.com

xlv History.com

xlvi Great Negroes Past and Present by Russell Adams

xlvii Womenshistory.about.com

xlviii www.history.com

xlix www.biography.com

l www.history.com

li www.wikipedia.org

lii www.imdb.com

liii Great Negroes Past and Present by Russell Adams

liv www.american.edu

lv www.wikipedia.org

lvi www.artnet.com, www.askart.com

lvii www.biography.com

lviii Great Negroes Past and Present by Russell Adams

lix www.history.com

lx www.wikipedia.org

lxi www.biography.com, www.wikipedia.org

lxii www.history.com

lxiii www.biography.com

lxiv www.notablebiographies.com

lxv www.history.com

lxvi www.deion-sanders.com/bio

lxvii www.espn.com

lxviii www.espn.com

lxix www.biography.com, www.britannica.com
lxx www.biography.com
lxxi Teamusa.org
lxxii www.wikipedia.org
lxxiii www.wikipedia.org
lxxiv www.biography.com
lxxv www.wikipedia.org
lxxvi Whitehouse.gov,www.wikipedia.org

lxxvii www.wikipedia.com,ijr.com
lxxviii www.encyclopediaofarkansas.net
lxxix Great Negroes past and present by Russell Adams
lxxx Great Negroes past and present by Russell Adams

lxxxi Bioguide.congress.gov

lxxxii Bbcnews.com
lxxxiii www.wikipedia.com
lxxxiv History.com
lxxxv www.wikipedia.com
lxxxvi www.imdb.com
lxxxvii www.imdb.com

lxxxviii Biography.com
lxxxix Great Negroes Past and Present by Russell Adams
xc www.wikipedia.org

xci www.nicolelyonsracing.com

xcii www.britannica.com
xciii www.wikipedia.org

xciv www.jazz.org
xcv www.jazz.org

xcvi www.history.com
xcvii Blackpast.org

xcviii www.buffalosoldier.net
xcix www.civilrights.org
c History.com, www.civilrights.org

[ci] Blackpast.org, www.history.com, www.wikipedia.org
[cii] www.history.com, www.wikipedia.org , historynet.com

[ciii] Dale Carnegie Bronner, www.wikipedia.org ,
woffamilycathedral.org
[civ] Tdjakes.org, www.wikipedia.org

[cv] www.wikipedia.org , www.faithdome.org
[cvi] Worldchangers.org, www.wikipedia.org
[cvii] www.biography.com, pbs.org
[cviii] www.andraecrouch.org, www.wikipedia.org
[cix] www.imdb.com, www.mtv.com

[cx] Pbs.org, www.wikipedia.org
[cxi] www.wikipedia.org, www.mahaliajackson.us
[cxii] www.mtcalvarywordoffaith.org
[cxiii] www.biography.com, pbs.org
[cxiv] Chnm.gmu.edu, www.biography.com
[cxv] Articlebio.com, www.wikipedia.org

[cxvi] www.wikipedia.org

[cxvii] www.huffpost.com, www.wikipedia.org
[cxviii] www.biography.com
[cxix] www.ebony.com

[cxx] www.jetmag.com, www.wikipedia.org
[cxxi] www.essence.com, www.wikipedia.org

www.ingramcontent.com/pod-product-compliance
Lightning Source LLC
LaVergne TN
LVHW011218080426
835509LV00005B/198